SOUVENIRS
FROM
KYIV

BOOKS BY CHRYSTYNA LUCYK-BERGER

SECOND WORLD WAR

Souvenirs from Kyiv

The Woman at the Gates

The Girl from the Mountains

THE RESCHEN VALLEY SERIES

No Man's Land: A Reschen Valley Novel Part 1

The Breach: A Reschen Valley Novel Part 2

Bolzano: A Reschen Valley Novel Part 3

Two Fatherlands: A Reschen Valley Novel Part 4

The Smuggler of Reschen Pass: A Reschen Valley Novella – the Prequel

Chrystyna Lucyk-Berger

SOUVENIRS
FROM
KYIV

bookouture

Published by Bookouture in 2022

An imprint of Storyfire Ltd.
Carmelite House
50 Victoria Embankment
London EC4Y 0DZ

www.bookouture.com

ISBN: 978-1-80314-657-7
eBook ISBN: 978-1-80314-656-0

To my grandmothers, Olha Remenets'ka Lucyk and Maria Pundyk Smaha

Belarus

Russia

Poland

Luts'k · · Horodok

·L'viv

★Kyiv

·Kharkiv

Former
Czechoslovakia

Hungary

Moldavia

Rumania

FOREWORD

"GLORY TO UKRAINE!"

In 1991, 2004 and 2014, the Maidan in Kyiv was the stage for three major events that etched Ukraine into the European consciousness. These were the fall of the Soviet Union, the Orange Revolution and the Euromaidan respectively, the last of which ended in bloodshed but united generations of Ukrainians. Whereas the Orange Revolution succeeded in overturning a fraudulent election, the Euromaidan did nothing to change Ukraine's entry into the European Union (EU). For nearly four months, Ukrainians protested President Yanukovych's sudden decision to renege on his promise to make Ukraine part of the European Union, and instead bound Ukraine to Russia in the Eurasian Economic Union. Then, on February 24, 2022, the entire world not only understood Ukraine's existence but began speaking Ukrainian. Within a week, the words "Slava Ukraïni!" had been uttered by everyone from truck drivers to the world's leaders. Some copy and pasted the Cyrillic version —"Слава Україні!"—onto their social media posts. Whereas in World War II, nationalists and freedom fighters churned out handmade leaflets to boost morale, today we only need to turn to Twitter to get our hero-fix.

As a Ukrainian-American, I should be reveling in a bitter-sweet victory. From North America to Australia, from Asia to Africa, the world now recognizes that Ukraine is not Russia. In the span of just a few days, Vladimir Putin has accomplished what most Ukrainians the world over have been trying to do for nearly a century. As a first-gen American, I grew up defending myself and my heritage; a heritage passed firmly down by a family of displaced World War II refugees. "No, I am not Russian. Yes, Ukraine is a separate country. I speak Ukrainian. Why should I speak Russian? Does every Italian speak Spanish? Does every Portuguese person speak fluent French?"

The world will never forget what the Ukrainian flag looks like thanks to the landmarks and architecture illuminated worldwide in blue and yellow. An obscure president has risen to superhero status. TikTok videos propagate the high morale amongst Ukrainian defenders; videos feature young soldiers dancing with bazookas and Kalashnikovs. Street fighters teach viewers how to make Molotov cocktails and where to target for the best damage, or—better yet—if you don't have a tractor to tow one away, a young woman has created an instructional video on how to drive home a captured Russian tank. It's surreal when, from every corner of the world, we can watch David throwing stones at Goliath. And feel the suffering. Or at least imagine we do. In the process, we are glorifying Ukraine. We are glorifying the heroes born on social media. We are witnessing communities, a country, even a world stitched together by a common cause: to cheer on these blue-and-yellow underdogs. Thanks to Hollywood, we are conditioned for that happy end to arrive within ninety minutes. In war, it does not. And the impact is felt over generations.

I've spent my entire adult life trying to make sense of the horrors my relatives survived in World War II. During one of my interviews with her, my grandmother stopped and rubbed her face. When she looked back at me, she said very soberly,

"There was nothing glorious about our fight. I hope your generation never has to experience what we went through. Ever." And here we are. I spend my nights sobbing.

I write historical fiction for complex and deeply personal reasons. If I have to simplify it, then my mission is to recover and repair the stories we have lost so that we can reflect on how we have gotten to where we find ourselves. I write to build empathy. And I write to resolve the truth behind the big picture; to make it clear that conflict is not about two teams meeting on the battlefield—one called "good" and one called "bad." There are no winners in this story.

"Glory to Ukraine!" demands the response "Glory to the heroes!" But even that salute is not complete. There is a third part. It is "Death to enemies." I don't see many people posting that on their social media. Neither in English nor in Cyrillic. To understand the power of this salute, you must understand its history. Versions of it were used during Ukraine's War of Independence (1917–1921), and then it was adopted by a renegade partisan group in the 1940s, whose mission was to "purify" Ukraine of Jews, of Poles, of Nazis, of Soviets. It is a chant that was banned by Soviet authorities and resurrected in 1991 when Ukraine wrested itself from the USSR, and when her borders reappeared on world maps. Finally, "Glory to Ukraine!" echoed over the Maidan by a generation born into freedom, and has now become eternalized as Ukraine battles for its very existence during the Russian invasion. The salute is mired in blood and in sacrifice even as its meaning has shifted to unify an entire world. And maybe that is okay if the words are not lost in a vacuum; if the words—which mean so much—can be understood.

"Glory to the heroes!"

I was raised by freedom fighters. In the 1970s and '80s, "Nordeast" Minneapolis was a unique blend of Eastern European, German, Jewish, Lebanese, and Indian families. A Lebanese deli and a Ukrainian butchery became iconic in the Twin Cities. Two Ukrainian churches were located right across the street from one another: the Byzantine Catholic one and the Orthodox Christian one. My father belonged to the former, my mother to the latter. My relatives could not return to Ukraine because it was now the USSR and their family names were listed alongside a one-way ticket to a *gulag*. I grew up in a family whose story was anything but secret. Every time we were served bread, we were reminded of where we'd come from, and how very lucky we were to have that bread. These stories quickly gave me an unquenchable thirst for justice and for defending the "underdogs." From an early age, I rooted for the Davids in this world, cheering them as they stood up to the Goliaths of the universe.

For the first two decades of my life, I had no idea that I was stewing in nationalism either, or what that even meant. This Ukrainian-American generation grew up in the lap of Ukrainian consciousness and we felt special because we spoke a language hardly any other American knew, and wielded knowledge about a country that few understood had the right to exist. Russia and Russian were curse words in our Diaspora. We learned "our" stories, "our" history and "our" heritage in Ukrainian schools that were held on Saturdays. We attended church every Sunday, because first came God, then family, and only then friends. We expressed our unique identity through Ukrainian folk dance, Ukrainian scouts, and went to Ukrainian summer camps where kids from Chicago and Minneapolis met in the woods of Wisconsin for three weeks and marched around singing rousing battle songs about freeing Ukraine from foreign enslavement. If you'd seen us, you'd think we were paramilitary. I wouldn't have understood what that meant. All I knew was that I was fiercely proud. Proud of my heritage. Proud of my people. Proud about knowing where I'd come from. We were all lying in wait for our moment when we would rise up, grab hold of our independence, and make sure the world knew Ukraine. We were waiting to be those glorified heroes.

Some will laugh. What were a bunch of Americans thinking they were going to do? Return to the home country? That is exactly the mentality our Diaspora instilled in us. When Ukraine regained its independence, first-gen Ukrainian-Americans left in a swarm to work as doctors, lawyers, teachers, and business people. People I'd grown up with were heading over to help reboot the country and make their parents and grandparents proud.

I was also feeling this wave of national pride but tackled it a bit differently. In the 1990s, I was studying journalism. When I realized that my grandmother and her siblings were aging, I started recording their stories with the intention of immortalizing them. Instead, I learned something that took my pride down several notches. Everything I thought I knew about my family couldn't even scratch the surface. My relatives were surprisingly forthcoming, but it would take me many decades before I felt I could do the stories justice. It was many years, many trips, and what felt like many lifetimes later that I began to understand what their struggles were about; what this fierce need for sovereignty and independence cost them. And now I share a cautionary tale: glorifying any country, especially one at war, is a delicate business. It can quickly create a one-sided fiction based on misinformation and misunderstanding; it can do more harm than good because the disappointment that comes afterwards is earth-shattering. The true story of the Ukrainian is not in the least bit a black-and-white tale; it is not even allegorical. It is human with all the fragility and strength and contradictions and complexities every human being carries within themselves. However, it is also a common story that connects us at the most elementary level: the need to be free.

"Death to Enemies!"

In 1945, journalist Edgar Snow pronounced that "World War II was a Ukrainian war." It is understandable why he would be compelled to do so. The Eastern Front had seen some of the most horrific, no-holds barred violence. Stalin and Hitler had both applied "scorched earth" policies, burning everything down so that the other side could not profit from any valuable resources.

During World War II, no Ukrainian could ever name just one enemy. No Ukrainian knew from day to day who the enemy really was. Stalin's and Hitler's armies were inarguably responsible for the slaughter of millions upon Ukrainian soil, but add to that the fluid infighting between Ukrainian political factions, and the result was rampant fratricide and blind hate. Partisan units fought and mass murdered locals whose ideologies were not the same and fell upon Poles, under whom western Ukrainians had been oppressed; and Ukrainians had a hand in the extermination and deportation of the local Jewish populations. Details were slow to come to the surface after the war, no thanks to the Soviet Union's lock-and-key policies, but when that information did trickle out, many exiled Ukrainians around the world were confronted by the ugly truths about their countrymen. Many were also given the opportunity to reconcile with their pasts. I, for one, was only beginning to understand things that sobered me. My community's stories were complex, shocking, real-life struggles for survival, and they came at heavy prices.

In 2002, I took the vast material I had and aimed to unravel the tangled roots born of Ukraine's role in the World War II. In

2020, I published six of those stories under the title *Souvenirs from Kiev*. It was my attempt to connect the world to Ukraine and Ukrainians, and to share my understanding of a lesser-known history. Now, Bookouture has offered to help get these stories into the hands of more readers than I could possibly reach alone. I took liberties with the characters and events in order to weave together a complete portrait of the Ukrainians that I have met, loved, and respected—of a culture and country that I have grown to better understand as I have matured, and to love ever more deeply. My romance with Ukraine has turned into a true and steadfast love; the more I learn about her fragility and faults, the more I embrace and accept her.

Russia has been trying to effectively wipe Ukraine off the world map for thousands of years. They haven't succeeded yet. And they certainly won't be able to now that the entire world knows the country's salute. I plead for peace in these pages, but that hybrid freedom fighter in me cannot deny this one very simple fact: by republishing these stories, I am picking up my stone and throwing it at Goliath. I am suddenly empowered to help make an impact. My mission has not changed: I want people to *understand*. To learn. To have their horizons broadened and to realize that there is no glory in war; there is no glory in the fight for survival. Instead, I turn to the brighter light found in the Ukrainian anthem:

Ukraine has not yet perished; not her glory, not her freedom

Fate shall smile upon us!

Our enemies shall vanish like dew in the sun;

And we too shall rule our beloved country.

I like to imagine Russians standing up to Putin and making

him draw back. Because if they do not—if *we* do not stand up to him—we have learned nothing from our previous mistakes. This spring, before our very eyes, a new world war is blooming, and it will not—I promise you—take on the shape and color of sunflowers.

Chrystyna Lucyk-Berger

Austria, March 2022

SOUVENIRS FROM KYIV

KYIV, 1942

The Herr Oberst came to me on a sunny afternoon just a week ago. I was tucking in the tails of my headscarf and eyeing the work I had in my studio: one embroidered shirt for a Wehrmacht soldier, who I have since heard terrorizes the civilians when he's drunk; another blouse, still sleeveless and with no embroidery, hung on the wooden makeshift mannequin. That one was for the German woman, who had transferred to Kyiv to be near her boyfriend. She came to me, dressed up in city clothing from the west and toting a pair of miniature Spitzes on leashes. She cooed to them as if they were precious, innocent children. The urge to kick them all—the woman and the dogs—was something I still have not come to terms with. Years ago, I would never have thought like this. Years ago, we lived in a fairy tale.

The Herr Oberst appeared in my workplace wearing a smart uniform. His dark hair was carefully groomed and parted to one side. His features were handsome but his gray eyes cut right through me. A *schuma* was also with him, a policeman I recognized from earlier years whose name is Chovnik. Ha! He calls himself one of us—*nashi*—but he is a rat! When the Bolsheviks took over this city, he licked their shoes with glee. When the NKVD ran rampant, he led one of their squads. Now, with Kyiv sealed off by the Germans, he slobbers on the boots of the Nazis. Anything for a piece of bread these days, which is as accessible as diamonds are to peasants.

He wanted one of my shirts, the German officer explained. Loot for the conquerors, I thought. What our traditional dress is to us—a symbol of identity—has become a novelty item in high demand.

For whom did he want the shirt? I asked.

For himself, he told me through the *schuma* interpreter, to be personally fitted and embroidered on the finest linen.

In bare feet, I took the Herr Oberst's measurements. He stood proud and still, as if he were being fitted for a suit by an Italian tailor and had reason to display his colors. His freshly shaven face gleamed the way his freshly licked boots did. These Germans! They take pride in their appearance but when we are on the streets, waiting for the infrequent trams, they do not see us. They pick their noses or pull their pants down to urinate on the sidewalks as if we are not there.

To measure for a shirt, I may start at the base of the neck and then measure across both shoulders. That's how I started with the German officer. Avoiding his eyes—avoiding looking at his face entirely—I moved to his front and pulled the tape from the collarbone to just below the waistline. I am a professional. Measuring men does not bother me but at that moment I was more than aware of his belt. The black cross. The Latin letters. I was aware of what lay below that belt, and my hands shook. Not from curiosity, or desire. From fear. Fear of the killer instinct within each of us. Our intuition rarely fails us, and I have crossed borders I never dreamed of in order to survive. You learn to depend on your intuition and—when you have nothing else—on your intuition alone.

When I was finished, I looked up at the *schuma*, who

tapped his baton into his other hand, pursed his lips and strode around my ruin of a workshop, wearing a path around the Herr Oberst and myself. I had no doubt he was ready to use it if need be. For what, it didn't matter. They never need a reason.

I noted down the two measurements and snapped the tape's edge between my fingers. Perhaps my movements were too sudden but when I reached up on tiptoe to wrap the tape around the Herr Oberst's neck, he jerked back. It was only a second. His eyes lost that steely confidence; they fired repulsion at me. My breath caught in my rib cage. I thought I might faint. Behind me, the *schuma* moved, but the German composed himself, raised a hand, and gave me the slightest nod. As I proceeded to measure the size of his collar, I knew that, as I reached for his neck again, we were all thinking of that lamp-post across the street. We were all picturing that boy the Nazis had hung from it last week.

Forty-six centimeters.

Beneath my scarf, my hair is cropped close to my head. When I look in the shard of mirror I have on the wall, I see hunger. Will Andrej recognize me? He calls me his green-eyed beauty, his princess. What princess must walk in bare feet as it gets colder? What princess cannot find a pair of stockings to purchase? What princess is dressed in layers to protect herself from the hungry stares of the predators outside? This has been my costume since we have become familiar with the Nazi's lust for rape. Yet, it isn't so much the Germans who do it. No, they simply kidnap women who are on their way to work, and send them to the brothels. Gentlemen, all of them when they—the Germans—invaded the borders to the east. The closer they moved to Ukraine's center, the closer they became familiar with their darker halves. Harmless compared to the Hungarians however, who have also dressed up in Wehrmacht uniforms to justify their thirst for blood.

No, the Germans are known to go to bed with Kyivan women, and that is how the girls have learned to eat. Many of the girls now have foreign boyfriends and sleep in comfortable beds and eat twice a day. I overheard a conversation on the street between a German and a local woman once. She invited him to have tea with her but he simply ignored her.

She continued to press him then, with unmasked anger, she said, "Is it not true that the Germans like to rape us? Am I that ugly that you would not have a piece of this?"

The boy turned his face away and spat on the ground. "As you see," he replied coolly, "it is not we who harass you but you who harass us."

For embroidery, the traditional colors of Kyiv are red and black. Sometimes we use gold and green—influences from Galicia— and other colors depending on the style one wants. I pulled out a few patterns for the officer to look at.

"What patterns would the Herr Oberst like," I asked the *schuma*. I listened to their rough tongue, catching a few words that had become familiar to me. To all of us.

"The Herr Oberst," the *schuma* snarled, "wants something special. He believes you're some kind of artist."

That the German should know this surprised me. It is true. I was a painter before I took up embroidery. In Kyiv, I am known for my original work, mixed with traditional stitching and patterns. I have served the *intelligentsia*, politicians' mistresses, and foreign men and women in prominent positions. I have sewn and embroidered costumes for entire choirs and dance troupes. Pride—though one of the deadly sins—is what makes my work stand out in this city, and it must have been pride, which spurred me to say, "If I'm to do this properly, I must know *exactly* what the Herr Oberst expects."

The *schuma* grinned and tapped the baton in his palm. "He leaves that up to you. And if it is not unique, not representative of the country the Germans have conquered..." *Tap. Tap. Tap.*

The Herr Oberst was watching our exchange with an amused look. At that point, he walked around the workshop—a quarter of the size of the one we'd had in the Sophia district. The Sophia and the Pecherska districts have been closed off to the civilian population and the houses requisitioned by our current occupiers and their guests. I am not even sure whether the workshop still stands after the Great Fire of forty-one but I imagine that it is still there and that two Spitzes probably sleep inside.

"I want a souvenir," said the Herr Oberst in Russian.

The *schuma* reached into his canvas satchel. He tossed a paper parcel onto the table. When I opened it, the materials I would need—the linen, and the needles, and the thread—were all inside.

He has given me two weeks, with the promise that he will pay in reichsmark. These days, I get paid a pittance for my shirts, for my blouses, and the skirts. A pittance for my art. Often, I am simply paid in grain because our money is no good anyway. We cannot afford to exchange for reichsmark. *If he pays me in reichsmark...* My imagination conjures up a table full of food.

This is how we eat: we trade, we beg, we stand in line for millet and a piece of fat with no guarantee of getting anything at all that day. So, sometimes, and at great risk, we steal. It's never enough. I fear that my craft is fading with the body which completes it. These days I do not care so much about how my work gets done, only that it is done. And still, I fight with myself to make sure that there is dignity and beauty in my work. It is a contradiction of emotions just as this war is a contradiction of two enemies fighting over our ever-emptying breadbasket. And we are the hosts standing helplessly by.

The *schuma* came back to see if I had started. The days are shorter and at night we have no light. When I showed him what I had completed, he beat me. Not hard. Hard enough. Later, he returned with wicks and oil and black paper for the windows so that I can work despite the blackout order.

Mamusia—my poor mother—brings me millet soup twice a day. Yesterday, the German woman sent her maid to pick up the blouse which I'd finished up in a hurry. I was paid in a sack of potatoes; it was half the cost of what we had agreed upon, and the servant gave me a weak excuse that it was all the good Frau could get. I was furious, but I did not take it out on the young girl. Instead, I gave the potatoes to my mother, who pressed her hands to her chest, and kneaded them where her heart was as if she were trying to get it to work again. I told her to feed the others and to bring me the usual soup.

Food is a constant cross on our backs now that the city is an island, isolated from the ravaged land beyond. Our markets are ordered closed at a second's notice and prices are ten times higher than our wages. The peasants from the countryside no longer come. It was on them that we had relied upon for food supplies. I did not tell Mamusia where the potatoes had come from. We all know. We all know where they come from, and we can only guess what blood has been shed for those roots torn from our ground. Torn from *nashi liudy*—our people.

How my family and I survive is no small matter, and you must know that we are not proud of what we do to manage. Our city is dwindling. After the Nazis shut down all the schools from the fourth grade upwards, my twin brothers qualified as workers for the Fatherland. Under Stalin we had lived as workers for the Motherland. The twins were deported to Germany as *Ostarbeiter* and we have not heard from them for over a year. We do not know whether they are alive. When they left, they were twelve.

My family. What remains of us? My father is ailing, and he begs the merciful Lord to take him. My sisters, Slava and Petrusia, are sixteen and eighteen, with no future. They have been working at the soap factory since the Academy of Sciences was also shut down. I am twenty-six years old and married. I do not know where my husband Andrej is. He is a tailor as well. My last memory of him is of him sewing a photo of me inside his Red Army uniform by lamplight. That short night, we did not sleep but clutched one another as if we would be carried away on the storm that rushed at us. A storm of wind, and water, and fire.

Andrej and I had a workshop with six employees. They, like him, were scattered to those winds when the battle over Kyiv broke out and I do not know where any of them are now.

I do know where our son is. Sasha is in heaven.

There is a poster on the wall somewhere. I cannot think of where exactly at this moment, though I pass it every day. It is a colorful piece of art. It shows five Eastern Europeans, Slavs —*Untermenschen*, as the Nazis call us—standing at a large hole in a wall. They are looking at a view to the west. A train, churches, a village, a factory—wealth—all accessible beyond this distance. In Ukrainian, the poster reads, "The wall has come down! Stalin has hidden from you the pitiful state in which you live. Your salvation is to the west!"

In 1941, the Germans invaded and tore down Stalin's wall.

We welcomed them with salt and bread. We threw flowers on their tanks and invited them to our weddings. We danced in the streets and fought the Great Fire with them. Together, we cursed the Bolsheviks who planted bombs in our most beautiful buildings and caused that fire. Then, when we got comfortable, the Germans built up a new wall.

If we tore this wall down, we would see a much greater sight than trains and villages. We would see farms with an abundance of food and that food would be collected, stolen, ripped from the children's mouths and shipped to the west or to the front lines.

"Let the Red Army come back," I hear. "They might shoot us as well but only half of us."

I pull the stitch tight on the blooming red border. Inside is where I will embroider the motifs and fill in with black, with gold, and with green.

Andrej and I met on the banks of the Dnipro River during the Ivana Kopala festival. It is the day when women twist flowers and long grasses into wreaths. We sing songs and speculate over our sweethearts, then drop the wreaths at dusk into the river with the hope that this will be the day we finally find our true love. The boys then fish out the wreaths and seek their owners. I had hoped that Andrej would find my wreath. It was woven with poppies and cornflowers, daisies and lupin. I was wearing my newly embroidered blouse with large red poppies stitched onto the sleeves. When he returned from the banks with my wreath, my heart pounded so much I was sure everyone could hear and see it. We stood and blushed at one another, and then he put his hand in mine and we did not let go of one another for the rest of the night.

The next week, he came to our family home in the Pecherska district, a bouquet of poppies in one hand and the promise of love in the other. My girlfriends were delighted but my two other suitors laughed amongst themselves. Andrej is different, some people say. Soft, perhaps. Romantic and dreamy, but a hard worker. And he doesn't drink. He has never lifted a hand against me.

On our wedding night, he carefully unrolled the crown of braid on my head. "Larissa," he whispered, "you are a woman now. Only girls wear braids." And he unwound my hair until it lay flat on my back.

With caresses, he led me to the bed and instructed me to sit in front of him. Then he brushed my hair with gentle strokes until it shone like a raven's wing under a full moon. He kissed the nape of my neck as if he were kissing a feather-light poppy under a hot June sun.

I lost my breath in him. I learned to breathe through him.

A woman's blouse is delicately embroidered around the collar. Two strings with pom-poms are used to tie the slit closed which begins at the collar and goes down to the cleavage. The edges of the tapered wrists also contain a simple pattern. The real artwork on a woman's blouse is on the puffed sleeves. There, the pattern can be as feminine or as rash as suits the wearer's character and taste. I usually make the embroideries first and then stitch them onto the blouses, or the dresses, or the skirts. If it is a more expensive shirt, I stitch directly onto fine linen. This requires full concentration and allows for few errors. Men's shirts have elaborate wide embroidery along the front slit (to about the breastbone) and follows on up around the entire collar. The wrists are also more thickly decorated. I usually spend two or three days with the person who will wear my work so that I may find a little of what touches their soul. I don't need this time with the Herr Oberst. I already know what will affect him. The best art is the kind that causes one to self-reflect.

I am working on the Herr Oberst's collars. The wrists are already complete. I will not allow him to take souvenirs of our country back with him, rather the impressions he will leave behind on us. The wrists are embroidered like this: I used red to create a barbed-wire pattern and inside that are the black lightning symbols of the "SS."

The first Red Army POWs were captured and led through the streets in a procession the way Jesus had been led through the city of Jerusalem. Instead of wearing crowns of brambles on their foreheads, the prisoners trickled blood from their wrists where they were bound together by barbed wire. Frantic, I searched for a glimpse of Andrej, and I saw that some of our people, *nashi*, spat on the prisoners. I could not believe it. Collaborators! They call themselves Nationalists. They believe Hitler will hand them over a free Ukraine. Murderers and thieves are what they are.

Others, mostly women, threw bread and tried to give the prisoners water, but they were often beaten back by the parade of rubber batons. One woman, who had defied a sharp "Halt," was simply shot in the head by a German soldier on horseback.

I did not find Andrej among the prisoners, and for the first time in a very long time, I made the sign of the cross in the open.

The prisoners were pushed toward the outskirts of Kyiv, toward Babi Yar where we hear their bodies rest in a mass grave. Now, we wonder, when will the Red Army push back?

I am now working above the sheaves of wheat at the end of the collar, near the breastbone. They are bundled by the Third Reich's insignia, black on gold. The next motif is a poppy, hanging upside-down above the wheat. Above the poppy will be a wreath of flowers draped over crosses. Not the Orthodox crosses of my country. No. It is the same as the cross that hangs around the Herr Oberst's neck and every other high-ranking SS officer.

When the first German soldiers were buried in 1941, we women went to the graves with flowered wreaths and we wailed and lamented for the fallen. We cried and sang, "You poor lad! You fell so far from home, on foreign soil. What will your mothers know of you now? How will they suffer never knowing where their son lies buried?"

As I wiped away the last of my tears and led Petrusia and Slava back home, we passed a group of Wehrmacht soldiers standing about, smoking cigarettes and shifting from one foot to the next. They looked everywhere but at us. They were dumbfounded by our grief. They were dumbfounded because our grief was real.

Bat'ko never awoke this morning. Petrusia fetches me because I fell asleep in the studio. We walk in silence back to the space we share with two other families. I am relieved during the walk back and numbed when I see my father's body lying on the bed. Mamusia sits on the edge, next to him, her hand covering his knotted fists. They were good to one another.

I am swept away by an old vision I've had of growing old with Andrej, perhaps in the little *dachka* we dreamed about, with a garden. Now I feel the tears. Now I break down. And even as I sob, it is not for my father that I am grieving. My father faded away months ago. I am crying for selfish reasons. I am crying over that old dream.

We have to get permission from the commissar to bury Bat'ko. It is difficult to find a priest. I have instructed Slava and Petrusia to weave a wreath of black-eyed Susans and gerberas. It's too late for poppies. And we have no wheat for his grave. We cannot nourish my father's broken spirit in the afterlife either.

I sit here, like an empty shell now, back in my studio, and wait. Waiting for nothing.

The Herr Oberst's souvenir is ready. I sense the rat's presence under my door before he even knocks. I would be lying if I said I wasn't nervous. Terrified even. This is the best work I have ever done in my life. Of this I am certain and yet there is no joy in that knowledge.

They both come in. The shirt is hanging on the wooden mannequin.

"Heil Hitler," they both bark.

The *schuma* motions me aside and the Herr Oberst approaches the shirt.

I can't breathe. My head is spinning, but I grab hold of a chair. *Larissa*, I hear Andrej say, *this is what you were born to do. This is how you express yourself.* That is what he would have said. His voice still sounds in my head, but it has grown faint.

The German fingers the sheaf of wheat at the base of the collar and I see a smirk as he notes the swastikas that bundle them. Above that is the poppy, then the German cross with the wreath. After that, instead of the dove of the Holy Spirit above the German grave marker, I embroidered an eagle, flying sideways and up, its wingtip touching where the Herr Oberst's collarbone would be. It looks similar to the eagle on the sleeve of his uniform jacket. After the eagle, the motif around the rest of the neck is that of a braided rope. At the back of the neck, exactly in the middle, are two nooses touching one another, and then the whole pattern begins down and along the other side of the collar. All of this is captured within a row of "SS" insignia on the inside and the outside.

He is inspecting each motif closely and I hear him grunt as he moves from the collar and lifts the two ends of the sleeves. He swings to face me, disbelief written on his face. The *schuma* jumps, ready to obey his snake charmer's next tune. I am aware that my apathy may be too arrogant, too courageous for them both.

"Creative," Herr Oberst says in Russian. "Unexpected."

The sleeves slip from his fingers, and a sound comes from deep inside the German colonel. He looks at the collar again, and then he starts to laugh.

Chills overrun my body and I am shaking. I prepare to defend myself, but he turns on his heel and faces me and the rat.

"*Sie ist wirklich eine Kunstlerin,*" he cries. And he continues laughing, as he touches and studies the shirt again.

The *schuma* faces me, looking as astounded as I feel proud. The enemy has understood what he faces.

"You," the German points at me, still chuckling. The wrinkles around his flint gray eyes are creased and even the *schuma* begins to smile a little. "You are artist! You capture history, and I take it. Yes, I take it before the Communists come back and claim it as their own souvenir."

His smile vanishes and he strides to the door.

I am quicker than my common sense. "If the Red Army is coming, really coming, then it's best you pay me before you flee."

The Herr Oberst stops but does not look at me. He locks eyes with the *schuma*. "Chovnik, pay her what she deserves."

He leaves me alone with the traitor.

"Pack up the shirt," Chovnik says, smooth like iced glass.

Still shaking, I do as I am told. The weavings of my past and my broken life are one motif now. I think of Andrej and how he may come home, but like me, he will never be the same. I think of the Germans picking up and fleeing, the Red Army laying claim to the scorched land, and I know that one oppressor is no better than the next. I finger the poppies before I finish wrapping the shirt.

A solid click brings me back to reality and I stare at the barrel of Chovnik's gun. Beyond it, I see his lips moving but I hear something else. I hear wind, and water and fire—I hear them all come on one blessed storm.

THE PARTISANS: PART ONE
MYKHAILO

Kharkiv, 1942

A soldier on leave is a soldier who is faced with the terrifying prospect of confronting himself. That is what I think as I board the connecting train that will take me back into Ukraine and away from the German-Russian front. Not until the train has picked up speed does it dawn on me that it is the day before Christmas Eve. For the Germans, that is. Ukrainian Christmas is not until January the sixth. I open the bag of post I am to deliver in Kharkiv and look inside: letters posted to relatives, women—perhaps lovers—and even priests. Some are to be mailed within Ukraine but most to German or Austrian addresses. *Frohe Weihnachten* is sometimes written on the envelopes. Our hands are constantly cramped from the cold and the handwriting sometimes looks childlike, even innocent.

I feel a nauseating pang of nostalgia and homesickness. When was the last time I'd heard any news from my family? I count backwards. Forty-one. Forty. Thirty-nine. It's been three years and there's been no word from them since the Blitzkrieg. I look out the grimy window and, as the train slips past Lake

Liman, I realize Ukraine has grown unfamiliar to me, especially on this eastern end. I realize how very far away from my old life I really am. How very far from myself I have become.

Suddenly, the landscape of vast fields and plains is broken and I have to look twice. An entire forest of birch crosses rises from the snow. A helmet rests atop each one.

A young Wehrmacht soldier points out the window. "That's where we'll end up," he says. "Michael, you hear me? That is where our families will find us."

I ignore the boy due to his presumptuous familiarity with me. My name is Mykhailo and not Michael. For the first time in months, maybe even years, I am alone with my thoughts and I don't have to think in German either. Those reflections drift towards my orders: report to headquarters, drop off the post, submit the names of the dead. Turn that long, cumbersome list into a report so that someone can glue photos onto funeral cards and write condolence letters. I was the one who witnessed their deaths. I could write those condolence letters myself. It's time the truth be told.

> *Liebe Mutter des Vaterlands! Heil Hitler!* As we waited for our weapons to thaw, your son took a bullet. He did not die a hero. He did not kill many Red Army troops. He was shot, and others have died of TB, frozen to death, or have simply lost hope. You may stop sending blankets. They go to the officers, anyway. You could send clubs and knives, for we have been forced to turn into primitive cavemen. Our weapons are useless in this frozen land.
>
> P.S. This war, *Mutti*, is not about Jews or Soviets or the Breadbasket or *der Lebensraum*. This war is nothing but a delicate game of survival until the thaw. *Heil Hitler!*

Fields of snow-crusted, dried-up sunflowers, taller than a grown man, follow the graveyard of birch crosses. Their heads are bowed as if sleeping under a crown of heavy snow. Or as if in reverence to the dead I have just passed. The farms are an indication that we are near the city limits. My division marched through Kharkiv just months before, but we saw little of it. This time, I may linger before we head for Stalingrad. This time, I will get a taste of civilization away from the front. This brightens my mood and I push the memory of the last few months further away, like we're trying to push the Red Army further east: the constant cold, the constant hunger and, in particular, the hell I have been living has torn at my soul.

Feeling ill, I move away from the window, from the draft, but something outside catches my eye again. I try to wipe the pane clean, but the smears are on the outside. There are small groups of people, shadows against the shapeless, white landscape. The only daylight comes from the sinking sun, a hazy, pale-pink spot on gray canvas. Some of the people are holding on to one another as they march through deep drifts. Others, bent against the blowing snow, are carrying scanty sacks over their shoulders. All of them are bloated from layers upon layers of clothing, as if they have dressed themselves in every piece of fabric they own. The speeding train suspends these scenes, leaving me with the impression that these humans are blobs of ink on a bleak horizon. As I am carried closer to the city, the groups get thicker, eventually turning into forced columns. Hands are wrapped in rags and feet are bundled to the knees with tattered fabrics.

"Michael?" It's the boy again. He sounds fascinated and frightened. "Where are these people going? The city's been closed off."

This is news to me. I shrug, still looking out the window, and as we pull into the Kharkiv rail yard, the strange figures disappear completely, replaced by smartly-dressed Wehrmacht soldiers. When the train stops, I spring in front of the young soldier and, on the platform, submerge myself into the sea of gray uniforms. The boys are all heading towards the *Soldaten-heim* but I press through to the city gates, anxious to become a local. I salute a guard and he steps back as if I have just electrocuted him. The streets inside the city are empty and the light is fading by the minute. Down the snow-crusted vein, the alley opens onto a square. Life appears in the form of two bundles heading in my direction. As they come nearer, I see that they are two women. Judging from their smooth skin, they ought to be young but their eyes are haunted and their faces are pale.

"*Suchen Sie Übernachtung?*" one of the girls asks, her look falling on the valise in my hand. Her voice is tipped with weary but solicitous hope.

I am surprised to hear them speaking German at all. "*Wo ist Ihr Haus?*"

The taller one turns to her companion and switches into Ukrainian. "He wants to know where we live, Anna."

The girls must know only enough German to offer the exchange of a warm body for a crust of bread. I feel my throat clench and, instead of letting them know I am one of them, I motion that they should lead the way.

By the time we reach the small building where the girls must live or have use of a room, it is dark. From the bottom of the staircase, I can see the flickering light of a flame. When they lead me into the apartment, I am standing in a small kitchen, where an old, sullen man and his wife look up from the table and meet me with guarded looks. The oil lamp is pressed up against the wall, its rays revealing little. None of them ask me anything, as if I am not there.

The young girls shed their layers and they are so thin that their heads are disproportionate to their bodies. They might be beautiful though, with long, blond braids and wide, blue eyes. The older of the two catches me staring at her and gives me a look as if she knows what my first impressions of them are. I turn my attention to the valise I carry and set it on the table. The old man and the old woman sit back in their chairs, as if they expect the bag to explode.

As I take off my gloves, I imagine their surprise when I open it but the mother pushes herself out of her chair before I can unbutton my overcoat. She motions the girls to the stove, where a battered pot emits a light steam. I smell no food. Only mildew. Like two birds, the girls hover by the old woman with their mouths open to the spoon in her hand. I can see that there are no more than a few bits of cooked grain. The mother's eyes dart to me then back to the pot. She moves between the two daughters and me—the German-uniformed soldier standing in her kitchen.

Now is the right time to remove the contents of my bag, one at a time. The old man's unshaven chin sags under his open mouth. The girls turn away from the stove and, with an intake of breath, the air is charged by excitement. I continue removing the items—the sausage, the butter and, lastly, the bottle of cognac.

The younger girl exhales at last. *"Mamo,"* she says, "he has bread."

I open my arms to them and finally speak, my last surprise revealed. "Please," I say in Ukrainian, "please, come and eat."

At first none of them move except to lay their eyes on my face. They search it. The old man moans softly and his wife folds her hands and mutters something. I repeat the invitation, and this time everyone drifts to a chair. I pull up a stool for myself and encourage the old man to pour the French cognac. As we pass the food, there is still silence, and I notice that my hosts are making cautious examinations, taking hesitant nibbles, so I tuck in and begin shoving bread and sausage into my mouth. The old man grins widely. Then, the wife. Then they all laugh; a laugh I have heard lunatics make. They cannot stop.

Tears roll down their cheeks, mouths open, all four of them as if they are catching and passing this madness from one to the other. When the old man wipes his eyes, he must see that I am uncomfortable for he begins making apologies.

"It's just," he says, still trying to catch his breath. "It's simply that we have not had anything *good* to eat for... well, a long time."

The old woman nods, and her smile is bashful, as if she is ashamed for having protected that pot of nothing on the stove.

"God bless you," I say, and cut more slices from the meat. Even the oil lamp seems to burn brighter. "I am Mykhailo Hanchar," I say. "From Horodok, in the west."

The old man introduces himself and invites me to call him Pan Alexander, and his wife, Pani Valia. The younger daughter is Anna and the oldest, Natalia. They are cautious about eating too much and Pan Alexander, before clamping down on an empty pipe in his mouth, puts a hand on the bread and pushes it back towards my valise.

"How do you come to be here tonight?" he asks.

"It's a long story." I pour more cognac.

"Then start at the beginning," Natalia says, but it is not a warm request. She is still suspicious of me.

"I left my family in Horodok on St. Andrew's night almost five years ago," I start. "My brother-in-law and I fled the Communist NKVD, which was conducting a *chystka*."

"A cleanup." The old man purses his lips. "Of Ukrainian nationalists?"

I nod. "Months later, our teacher and my brother-in-law found us and asked whether we wanted to join a convoy going to Germany. The Germans were recruiting volunteers to work in their factories." I look up and they are all watching me.

Pan Alexander is sucking on his smokeless pipe. I reach into my coat pocket and the cigarette case I hold out to him looks garish against the background of poverty before me. The old man reaches with blackened fingers to take one, strikes a match and lights it. He holds the light to my own cigarette.

The women are waiting so I continue with my story. "My brother-in-law and I were sent to a furniture factory. Shortly after, I received a letter ordering me to report to the German infantry."

Pan Alexander frowns. "Why did you not simply return home? To Ukraine?"

It is a good question but my words, like my glass, are empty. "Because I believed that we would liberate Ukraine from the Russians. I believed that the Germans meant what they said with this," and I point to the insignia on my belt buckle. "God is with us."

Anna leans across the table, her eyes wandering over my chest. "What is that medal for, Pan Mykhailo?"

"We were surprised by a division of the Red Army that ambushed us in Andrijevka. That's where we're stationed now, and we're waiting for reserves. On this day," I lift the medal, "my whole division was almost wiped out. It was a cold, cold day and our panzers were frozen over. We prayed the Red Army would sit it out. Instead, they came on skis, silent, camouflaged in white. When the attack came, we were forced into hand-to-hand combat."

Anna nods and looks impressed but a reprimanding look from her sister evaporates the hint of a smile like smoke.

"So, were you at Kyiv when you, I mean..." Pan Alexander starts. "When the Germans, took the city?"

Was it really just three months ago? I feel as if the loss of our capital happened years ago. Yes, I say, and realize that to explain what happened at Kyiv, I must start at the beginning again.

"For training, our division was moved to the village across the River Bug, right on the Ukrainian border. On the other side, the Soviet Fifth Army had their base and went about their normal training routines. After all, the Germans had signed a pact to never attack. So, I was even able to visit friends on the other side in between exercises. We launched rubber boats across the river; we planned strategies and learned bomb-building techniques. This all seemed to me routine and mundane. Then we were told that Hitler declared war against the Russians."

I tell them about the Blitzkrieg, about crossing the Bug with the First Panzer group. I tell them about that scary sonofabitch, Kleist, and how we met up with Stülpnagel's Sixth Army at the Polish border.

"The Fifth had no idea that we were attacking them the next morning," I start. "And because of that, they didn't put up a fight. Before noon, we had hundreds of our Red Army friends arrested. Among them was my cousin, Petrus. It was the first time I had seen him in years." I shake my head, remembering holding him, hugging him to me, wondering how we had ended up like this. "What irony," I say aloud. "There we were, in two different, foreign uniforms, fighting over Ukraine."

Pani Valia sighs, mutters something about how the good Lord should protect us, and puts a hand to her face.

I want them to understand. Maybe I even want absolution. "I went to my commander and asked him to let Petrus join our side. He told me there was nothing he could do for me but that I shouldn't worry. He told me that they would be allowed to go home. What did he know? That was the last time I saw my cousin." I clear my throat. "They marched us all the way to Kyiv right after that."

Pan Alexander's voice has a slight edge to it when he asks, "And you continue to fight with the Germans?"

"Of course I do. Why wouldn't I?"

"Against your own brothers?"

"Against the enemy uniform," I correct him. "The same way

they fight me." I fold my arms over my chest. "Listen, I can't desert. They will kill my family. That is, if..."

"I am certain they are all right," Pani Valia offers. "The west has not been affected as we have."

There is an uncomfortable silence again, so I say, "I heard there was a legal Ukrainian army. Is that right?"

"The Ukrainian army didn't last long," Pan Alexander says. "They were destroyed at Kyiv."

"But how did the Soviets manage—?"

"Not the Soviets. It was destroyed by the Germans."

He has it wrong. "The Ukrainian army was German-authorized."

"It was too much for the Nazis to control and I tell you, son, *they* destroyed it. The only Ukrainian army now is underground. The only real Ukrainian army, Mykhailo, is the partisan."

Partisan!

The old man's head bobs up and down but his eyes are fixed on me. "They were supposed to be our liberators, eh? We thought these Nazis would give us jobs, so that we could help keep the Soviets out. In return for some food. We have been starving for almost a decade. The famine, you know? The Red Army was burning everything when the Germans pushed back. So, we welcomed Hitler's Wehrmacht with half-open arms, especially after we heard about the destruction of Kyiv. We just let them march right in and we took in their soldiers. You could almost say we moved aside so it was easy for them to do what they have done to us."

He chokes and I can see the lump, the sob, as he swallows. I lift the bottle of cognac and he nods. I pour us each another drink.

Pani Valia puts a hand on her husband's arm before rising and motioning to her daughters. All three women evaporate into the shadows of the next room.

"My wife," Pan Alexander jerks his chin after her, "still fears we will be arrested for speaking out loud. She doesn't accept the fact that we are already prisoners in our own city."

I do not speak. He needs time.

When the old man starts again, he has his voice under control. "By trade, I'm an engineer. I worked for a tractor factory. My wife is a civil servant. Natalia was attending her first year in medical school, and our youngest, well, she just finished middle school." He chuckles but cuts it short as if the memory is too painful. "During the famine of thirty-two..." He stops. He stares at me. "You did not have to live through that. We never would have believed that we would face more inhumane conditions than those imposed by Stalin. We never thought the Germans, coming from a civilized western society, were as unmerciful and cruel."

"What have they done to you?"

"When the German troops first came, they allowed us to leave the city limits. I took some of our clothing and exchanged it for food in the country, you know, bread, some horsemeat, grain, flour. I was lucky when I returned to the gates because I met a German guard who still had some sort of humanity left to him. Orders were to not let anyone with foodstuffs into the city. He was one of the very few who ignored our bulging pockets and pretended not to see the odd shapes under our coats. There were not many of us who made it back inside the day they closed the gates. This family is grateful to that soldier because we are still alive, but we're down to the last bits of grain."

The collar of my shirt has grown tight and I rub a finger underneath it, and clear my throat. I still feel as if I am choking. "I saw many people along the railroad tracks. Columns of them."

The old man nods. "Some are looking to get food to relatives inside the city. They wait for the trains of soldiers and officers, hoping that they will throw something out the windows."

I imagine the windows from the train. They'd been locked. I imagine the desperate hands that made those smears on the panes, begging soldiers to give them something.

Pan Alexander keeps talking, coughing in between at times. "Some of them are those that never returned in time and are still trying to get back in. They will probably only find that their relatives could no longer wait and have died from hunger and cold."

"Where do they go, then? Where do the people stuck outside the city go?"

"They die," the old man says, as if to say what other choice would there be.

"But who buries them all?"

"The snow, my son. The snow."

The next morning I share my food with the family again, and this time we eat with more ease because I promise them that I will smuggle more food from the *Soldatenheim*.

"I'll walk with you to into the city," Pan Alexander says, waving a forkful of sausage. "I'd like to show you something."

After breakfast, we take to the icy, cobblestone streets. It is a clear, sunny day, which only makes the air colder, especially in the shadows—of which there are many. I notice people drifting in and out of my line of vision in the alleyways, heavily bundled in tattered rags and old coats, scarves pulled so far over faces that I cannot distinguish the men from the women. They look the same as the wanderers I saw along the railroad tracks yesterday. All around me, people cough.

Pan Alexander says, "Mykhailo, have you noticed there are no cats or dogs?"

"Now that you mention it."

"Or rats?"

I shake my head.

Pan Alexander's smile is grotesque. "We ate them all."

We reach the headquarters where I am to complete the roll call of the dead and I hurry through the reports, afraid the old man could be harassed by the milling, bored soldiers outside. I manage to get through my work for the day, and my leave is approved. It allows me another four days before I must head back for the front, though none of what I had hoped to experience in Kharkiv—a homecoming amongst my countrymen—will happen now.

When I step back into the blinding sunlight, I see that some of the soldiers have built a fire. Two are passing a flask between them. Another stares at the fire and softly begins singing. I imagine it is a Christmas carol. Pan Alexander rises from an iced-over bench when he sees me. The two worlds I am moving in—the German Army and this city of ghosts—are more obvious to me. I stand in great contrast to my wild-eyed host. On the train, I believed I was ill. My condition is vibrant in comparison to his and I feel out of place in a city struck by a horrible parasite, a parasite which I—in my uniform—help to carry and spread.

"Where are you taking me?" I ask, looking towards the rail yard. Perhaps I should take my leave elsewhere. Home is two days away. I could go there, check on things. Then I would have to turn around and come back, or risk being arrested, maybe executed. My superiors would brand me a deserter.

"I'm taking you to the prisoner's camp."

I miss a step, but I know he does not mean anything else than to have me see it. Something drives me forward, a dark macabre side of me I seem unable to avoid. I've seen many prison camps; every German encampment eventually sets up a holding area for the captured Soviet soldiers, and we're good at capturing them. I wonder what the old man could possibly show me that I haven't already seen. I follow him along to the edge of the city and then I remember what I did not tell him last night.

"At the very beginning of the war, the Soviet Army did not want to fight. Many of them, of course, were Ukrainians, and they crawled out of their tanks without firing a shot. They gave themselves up to the Wehrmacht and hoped that they could turn around and fight the Soviets with them. So, the Germans—"

"Took them as prisoners," Pan Alexander says. He sounds annoyed. "And the strongest were sent to the front in German uniforms." He stops in front of a building, just before an alley. "Yes, Mykhailo," he says, "the same thing happened here. But the prisoners you will see here are civilians. They are our city's fathers and sons who resisted the Germans or have, since, caused them trouble in one way or another."

When we reach the end of the alley, I see a large fenced-in area. It could be a square or a paved playground but the snow-covered earth reveals no details. There are two dilapidated buildings on either end of the lot with hardly a thread of smoke coming from their chimneys, and piles of rubble and debris along the outside parameters. In between and against the fenced barriers are groups of men huddled together. They are bedraggled, torn, haggard, and I see that some wear no shoes or socks. Others are wearing only light, summer trousers. Most of them are half-naked in one way or another and all of them are under the bare, blue sky in below-freezing temperatures. Worst of all, I see that many of these stickmen are sitting on others who must have fallen onto the snow. Now they serve the living by keeping them off the cold ground. Some stare in my direction, but they are blinded by starvation.

I, too, feel frozen to the ground. I feel nothing. This is a problem. This is a horrific condition to be in.

I stare at the old man and finally my blood is moving again.

What do I say? That I am appalled? That, all this time, I have been wrong?

How very wrong you are! That is what his grizzled grin says, the way he looks at me from the edge of madness. "All of us will end under a mound of snow, Mykhailo. But those there? Those, inside? They may resort to what some did in the Holodomor and feed off one another."

He glances at me, at the prisoners behind me, and then at my valise. He suddenly looks frightened. "It's time for us to go back." He does not wait to see if I will follow.

I forgot to take the food from the *Soldatenheim.* My valise is empty. I turn to the fence again, and I feel something harden in the middle of my chest, then rise up on a swell of panic. If my bag was full, would I give these prisoners what it contained? If my bag was full, would I risk being shot by the guards to give these half-living corpses a taste of bread? But my valise is empty. I do not have to make that decision. I turn to catch up to the old man who, I know, is afraid that I will give the prisoners what he believes ought to go to him. I am surprisingly frightened of him. I'm frightened of what he could do to me.

In Kyiv, I thought I'd seen what hell was like. The most modern technology in warfare can rip apart not only the ground or buildings but human flesh into unrecognizable pieces. Those weapons destroyed the human body, but not always right away, and I have crawled and crept past many outstretched, bloodied arms, and voices begging for mercy. That is war. As soldiers, we are trained to anticipate that. But something worse is now tearing away at my soul, fragmenting it into unrecognizable pieces, and I am struggling to remain composed, to remain together at all. Having put on that German uniform, I believed that I stood on the side of those who fight for God, and those who respect the human right to freedom. The Soviets are godless people. Or so I thought. With the Nazis, we had the opportunity to build a "New Europe" and to join the more civilized west. That was what I had talked myself into before signing a Faustian deal.

I do not follow Pan Alexander and I hear him calling my name before I am finally out of range. At the *Soldatenheim*, I fill the bag with food as I had promised. My first day of furlough begins tomorrow, and time is running out. Out in the streets again, my heart beats, *Get out! Get out!* Just as it does when the enemy is firing at us.

Before dark, it is Anna that I finally find.

"Take this," I say.

"Why won't you come?"

So, this is what shame feels like. "I've been called back to the front."

Her rag-covered hand takes the handle. I press the valise to her. "Be careful."

It sounds ludicrous. I want to say something else, but she reaches with her other hand and caresses my face.

Because of the scarf, I see nothing of her mouth, but her eyes reveal life, something of a smile. "God bless you," she says.

In the morning, I take the train heading west, heading home, and force myself to burn the scene outside Kharkiv into my memory. These wanderers are momentary survivors in the wintered steppes. *Nashi liudy*—our people. From *my* country. I feel a strong pull, tugging at me so hard I must lie down on the hard bench. As the stars appear on the cold, dark blue sky, I know that I am no longer Wehrmacht. I will go underground. I will fight for those beneath the snow.

THE PARTISANS: PART TWO
MARUSIA

Horodok, 1943

Luba Denehar stood with her parents and her siblings in the village churchyard in the gray hours of dawn. Before them, ten SS took their places, nervous as horses in a deep river. On the fringes, Luba heard whimpering as entire families—her friends and neighbors—were shoved before the firing squad. Why didn't anyone run? Why didn't they all rush these murderers? Tackle them to the ground? Where was the courage her friends and she had sworn to when they'd met in their secret hideaways? When they'd vowed to protect Ukraine with their lives? How could they if they were dead?

Luba's legs failed her.

The officer—Rauling was his name—shouted something in German.

"But we don't know where they are," Luba's father pleaded in response. The officer did not listen.

"They" were here. "They" were the recruits and the recruits were in this very churchyard. Including Sasha. Their Sasha.

A pistol fired and Luba jumped. Her father—to her right—fell. The question again. "Where are they?"

But nobody knew where the partisans were. The next cry was cut short. Someone else crumpled to the ground, sprawling forward. Luba felt a punch to her shoulder and cried out for her mother. She stumbled backwards. Her knees buckled beneath her. A red-hot poker thrust into her, just above the hip. Boots stopped before her face. She held her breath.

God, please take me. Take me now.

She lay as still as she could so that He could find her.

Horodok was located amid a network of roads radiating from the main road that bore most of the traffic to and from the city of Luts'k. Clusters of farmhouses and rolling fields with woods of oak, maple, and aspen lined the road. Horodok's village center contained a cluster of homesteads, a guesthouse, the school. In the center stood the church, whose bell rang every hour from dawn until dusk, its deep tone colliding with the bells from neighboring *selos*.

It was the silence of this bell that awoke Domka Hanchar from sleep. She nudged Ivan next to her.

He snored one last time, then grumbled, "It's Easter Monday. At the very least—"

"The bell," Domka said. "It hasn't rung."

Ivan sat up, rubbed his eyes, and ran a hand over his long, drooping mustache. He shrugged.

Who knows? That was what he was saying. Every day the Germans announced new ordinances. Perhaps the Germans had forbidden church now, too, like the Bolsheviks before them.

Her husband was out the door and heading for the barn before Domka had put on her thick woolen socks. She went out to feed the chickens, leaving the children to sleep a little longer.

The morning was chilly, but the sun promised to dry up the dew. Their farm sat on a gentle hill just north of the Luts'k road. In the distance, wild poppies and cornflowers dotted the grassland, spilling toward a clear creek that marked the border of their farmland. Each spring they planted potatoes, wheat, and corn. In late spring another field provided hay. She had a vegetable garden next to the house, providing them with all the tomatoes, cucumbers, zucchini, and cabbage they needed, but her flower garden was what Domka enjoyed the most.

The house itself was modest and contained ample room for the family. They had a barn and a stable. The Arabian horses, deeply appreciated for their beauty and strength, neighed in greeting from the stable. The barn sheltered their two pigs, their six cows, and their goats, including a set of new spring kids. Ivan's workshop took up the left side. Chickens and domesticated geese roosted under a separate roof next to the doghouse. Sheptyk's doghouse. It had been standing empty since the German shepherd's miserable death. Sheptyk had swallowed a chicken bone, and when he'd begun choking helplessly, Ivan had asked the farmhand to shoot the dog. The boy must have done it with his eyes closed because Sheptyk had been wounded, not killed. Before Ivan could finish off the job, the dog had fled into the woods. He had either choked to death or slowly bled to death.

A cuckoo called out in the field, but the murmuring and clucks of the hens pulled Domka's attention back to the barnyard. She heard the tinny sound of milk hitting the pail and her husband shuffling on the stool as he milked. As she scattered the feed, a movement on the far bank of the creek made her straighten. The hairs on the back of her neck prickled. She stared at Sheptyk. Had she dreamed him up just now? Or was it the devil? She made the sign of the cross to ward it off, but the dog did not disappear. Instead, he paced back and forth, watching her. He was about to sit, but then his ears pointed forward, and he froze in an attentive posture. His panting also halted as his nose twitched. His half-opened mouth seemed to pull into a jeering smile, the very end of his meaty tongue tasting the air.

Domka shivered. She shook the last of the feed from her apron, and when she looked back across the creek, the apparition was gone.

She thought to tell Danylo about it but immediately reconsidered. Her son had been so upset over the loss of the dog. Besides, she thought as she went back into the house, by the time she woke the children for their chores it would slip her mind. So many things did these days.

Back in her kitchen, Domka started breakfast. She was mixing the cornmeal with goat's milk when an animal barreled against the window. She screamed and the bowl shattered on the floor. Sheptyk was scratching and barking at the window like a rabid animal. Just as quickly, he dashed away. Domka stepped outside to watch him run towards the creek, eventually swallowed up by the dry grasses. This time she knew the fear welling in her was not about seeing an apparition or even a wild animal. She followed along the back of the house, stopped above the main road, and cocked her head. A humming from the Luts'k road. Engines.

Domka hurried back into the house and into the children's room.

"Danylo! Marusia! Get up! It's the Germans!"

Both children shot up in bed at the same time.

"Mother?" Marusia asked sleepily.

But Domka was like a drill sergeant, as if she had been practicing for this moment all her life. "Get up! Put on your clothes! Stuff your pockets with bread!" Then she ran to the barn as fast as her old legs could carry her.

～

Danylo leapt out of bed before Marusia could. She pedaled backwards as her brother shoved past her and dropped to his knees. He lifted the mattress and Marusia gasped as he withdrew a pistol.

"Where did you find that?" she asked.

"An old Bolshevik bunker," Danylo said.

She paused in her dressing to watch her baby brother stuff the weapon into his waistband and throw on his shirt. He had just turned ten earlier that year, but Danylo was aging before her very eyes.

On his way out the door, Danylo snatched up their older brother's guitar—Mykhailo had made it himself years before— and sat with it on their father's bench. Marusia had to admire him for a moment. It was as if he were prepared to take inventory of whatever pulled into their yard. But what would those Nazis be up to at six in the morning? No good. She knew that much.

Her father stepped outside the barn and headed for his toolshed as if nothing were happening. Her mother lingered in the barn door, looking stricken. Marusia was too afraid to speak, too afraid to ask what her mother and father knew. Her father returned with a hoe slung over his shoulder, as though he were about to head into the fields.

"Nobody will catch us in bed," he muttered as he strode past Danylo and her.

Marusia's mother hurried to her and must have suddenly decided it was necessary to button up Marusia's yellow cardigan. "Put some socks on, child. Make sure you put on something warm."

Marusia returned to her room and pulled on a pair of socks and boots under her black skirt. She could hear the engines climbing the hill to their house. She eyed a pair of Mykhailo's old trousers hanging on the hook on the door and decided against them.

When she stepped to the door again, Marusia could see that three motorcycles and a car had pulled into their yard. Ten soldiers—she counted—disembarked and milled around for a moment. Marusia's father was intercepted by one of the soldiers and led to the house. One man wore a different cap—an officer. He stepped into the yard and nodded at the buildings, the farm, the chickens and geese but paused when his eyes seared into Marusia and Danylo. He strode to the porch, another uniformed soldier following him. The first one motioned for the family to go inside.

The group gathered in the kitchen, Marusia's mother wringing her hands over a broken bowl of cornmeal while her father kept his eyes on the man in charge. The German scanned the room as if assessing its worth. Danylo stood next to her, and she kept a hand on his shoulder. Her brother was unpredictable at times. She also noted that the back door was open. There, just beyond that door, were the woods.

"I'm Commander Rauling," the man said in Russian, as if that alone gave him the license to disrupt their lives. "It's a beautiful home you have here."

He paused over the mess on the floor and made a clicking sound, then stepped over it. He left the kitchen, and Marusia shifted to stand behind the second-in-command, trying to shrink into the walls but where she could still observe Rauling moving from room to room. The whole house was a showcase, this was true, but what would Rauling want with it? Her father was a skilled carpenter. He made everything himself—from the beautiful inlaid boxes to the furniture and fixtures. He and his brother had built the house themselves, and then her father had gone and helped her uncle build his.

Rauling stepped out of Marusia's bedroom and entered the pantry. It was laden with the remains of their Easter meal: smoked sausages, eggs, the braided bread, *paska*, and—from the rattling of glass bottles now—Rauling had found her father's *medivka*.

He came around the corner, holding two bottles of the honey-accented vodka. "These any good?"

Marusia's father ran a hand over his mustache. "Try it."

"Is that an offer?" Rauling glanced at his companion, as if to gain confirmation. "Because we don't steal."

Marusia's father made a gesture. Her mother scurried off to the cupboard containing the glasses, but the officer halted her. Outside the window, Marusia saw soldiers rummaging through the shed, going in and out of the barns. They were looking for something.

"Business first," Rauling said.

The officer before her opened the leather-bound document holder. She could see it contained a list.

"Are you Hanchar?" Rauling asked her father.

Marusia craned her neck as inconspicuously as she could and read: *Denehar, Luba. Denehar, Mykola. Denehar, Nadia.* And the list went on.

Her friends. Their families. OUN-member families. The Gestapo was coming down on the Nationalists. Were Danylo and she on it too?

"I am," her father said.

Rauling looked pleased. "You have a son. Worked in Germany?"

The Germans were looking for Mykhailo. Heart tripping in her chest, Marusia remembered how Mykhailo had warned them that this day would come. But nobody knew where Mykhailo was. Nobody. It was the only way they could protect him.

Marusia tried to get her father's attention, to plead with him, but her father was already shaking his head.

"No." He indicated Marusia and Danylo. "These are my children."

Rauling's smile came and went. He regarded Marusia and her brother with casual interest and then frowned. "You and your wife are old enough for grandchildren."

"I'm nineteen," Marusia hurried. "And I have an older sister. Olia. She lives with her husband..."

"Ah. And where would that be?"

"You must be thinking of my cousin," Danylo spoke up. "Mykhailo is my cousin."

Marusia's heart stopped.

Rauling cocked his head. "You're telling me there is another Hanchar in this village with a son named Mykhailo?"

"Yes," Marusia's father said. "My brother."

"My cousin," Danylo repeated. "Mykhailo works in Germany."

"Worked," Rauling said.

Worked. Was drafted. Fought for the Germans. And deserted. Marusia could still recall the heated arguments between her father and Mykhailo. He would put the family in danger, her father had said. Her brother had not disagreed.

Rauling paced in front of her, looked at the list his companion held. "And where does this uncle of yours live?"

"Just across the field," Danylo said. "It's shorter if you cross the fields rather than drive back to the bridge. There's a plank we use to cross the creek. The fields are still dry too."

Marusia was horrified. Her brother was sending them to her uncle. And when Rauling discovered he'd been tricked, what then? The Gestapo would murder her uncle and his entire family. Then return and shoot them all as well.

When her father offered to show Rauling the way, Rauling shoveled Danylo out with him together with the German who had the list. Marusia ran to her bedroom window to watch them point towards Uncle Andrij's house. Below their farm, on the road, the daily traffic of horses and carts and pedestrians had increased. Did anyone not see that the Hanchar family was surrounded by Germans? Did anyone have the courage to help them?

Marusia returned to her mother, who was fidgeting with cleaning up the broken bowl in the kitchen. The back door was still open.

"Mother," Marusia urged. "Stop that. We have to run. They'll kill us all. Please."

Her mother shook her off with a bewildered look. "How, child? I'm an old woman. How do you expect me to run from these murderers here?"

"I don't know." Marusia clutched her mother's arms again. "We have to try. Please!" All she knew was that she was too young to die.

Her mother continued to resist, and Marusia fled to the front door, stopping just before it to listen to what Danylo and her father were saying to the Germans. She could hardly believe it when Rauling took his second-in-command and all but two of the Wehrmacht soldiers with them. Behind her, Marusia felt her mother hovering. Marusia hissed to Danylo to come back into the house.

"Sheptyk was here," her mother said.

Marusia faced her. "Sheptyk? That's not possible. He died."

Her mother pointed to the retreating Germans heading towards Uncle Andrij's house. "He ran in the same direction not half an hour ago. It was Sheptyk who warned me," her mother said. "And look. There is no smoke coming from your uncle's chimney."

Danylo stepped onto the porch. "I heard barking this morning," he whispered, gazing at his mother. "I knew it was Sheptyk. And I thought I saw him running towards Uncle Andrij's when the Germans arrived."

Marusia's father appeared and walked in. "Andrij and the family just passed by in one of the wagons," he muttered.

"We have to run, Father. Please," Marusia begged. "When they find Uncle Andrij's house empty..."

She eyed the two remaining soldiers in the yard. They were leaning against their motorcycles and one lit a cigarette. Their ease was unnerving. She pushed back into the house and went into the pantry, cut slices of the Easter *babka*, and stepped out. To her father, she whispered, "You and Danylo head for the fields. Mother and I will keep these two busy until it's safe to escape. We'll flee through the back woods."

The soldiers straightened when they saw her, and tossed their cigarettes off to the side. They smiled and took her offering, thanking her. She stood for a moment, trying to solve the riddle. One moment the men were hunters and she and her family were the game; the next they were perfectly civilized gentlemen, somebody's well-bred sons.

Marusia's father had barely moved when she returned to the house, but Danylo was speaking to him. She recognized the urgency in her brother's voice. Why were they still arguing? Debating? What was there to debate about?

"We can hide in the Bolshevik bunker," Danylo whispered as he casually leaned on the wall of the house. "Or go to Aunt Sainka's."

Her father nodded at her, just once. "Danylo and I will take the woods off the field," he said. "You and Mother leave through the back and meet us at Sainka's."

"Ivan—" Mother protested.

"Go now," Father ordered. He glanced at Marusia, then at the soldiers devouring the *babka*. "Keep these two busy until your brother and I are hidden in the fields."

Danylo and her father fetched their hoes, and headed towards the fields, barely looking at the soldiers.

"Go get the *medivka*," Marusia said to her mother, and returned to the pantry to fetch hard-boiled eggs.

She nearly ran into her mother on the way out again, and

she grasped her arms from behind to hold her steady. "Do it for Father. For Danylo. They need you now."

Her mother stepped out and approached the soldiers, who let out a little cheer at the sight of the spirits. Marusia was surprised to see her mother raise a shot glass herself and down the *medivka* in one gulp. In the field beyond, her father tilled a row, eventually disappearing from view as the stable blocked him from sight.

She barely turned her head to see where Danylo was, but one moment he was tilling the field; the next moment a wagon rolled past him and he was gone. Marusia saw the driver look down to his right. Was that the miller? She understood her brother had to be walking alongside the cart.

"Would you like eggs?" Marusia asked the two soldiers. She showed them how to hold their eggs so that they could knock them against one another and crack them. She spoke in rapid Ukrainian, knowing they could not understand, and laughed a little. Her egg remained whole, and the two soldiers laughed and jostled one another as they peeled their cracked shells.

Checking over her shoulder, Marusia saw her mother going back into the house. She, too, must have realized the men were gone. It was time for them to flee as well.

Marusia promised the soldiers she would bring more eggs so that maybe this time they could win, and they laughed, offering her a cigarette. She declined and stepped backwards toward the house. Inside, her mother paced before the open kitchen door, and she began to plead with Marusia again. But Marusia slung the sack she'd filled with the remaining eggs, sausages, bread, and even a bottle of the spirits, grabbed her mother, and pulled her out the door. The woods they knew so well quickly closed around them.

Marusia's aunt could not take them in. Of course not. Instead, Aunt Sainka and Marusia's cousin, Yosep, hurried them into the house, cleaned their cupboards of all the extra blankets, gave them more food, all the while retelling what Yosep had discovered from the villagers on his way to church. They had turned him away and sent him running for home.

"The first panzers arrived at Aunt Irena's house," Yosep reported. "All we know is that they have come to take our people away. The youth that have been involved with the OUN, and their families, everyone."

Marusia's mother moaned and made the sign of the cross over and over.

"I ran into some of the boys," Yosep said, pulling Marusia and Danylo off to the side. "They said that before dawn, they'd heard shots in the churchyard."

Marusia remembered the list. She swallowed back the tears. "What about Mykhailo? Do you know where he is?"

Danylo frowned at her and shook his head. "How should he know where Mykhailo is? Nobody knows where Mykhailo is."

Yosep shook his head. "I don't know whether he's still safe, but I heard that Sasha—"

"Volykh?" Danylo asked. "They got Sasha?"

Their Sasha. Their fearless leader.

Yosep nodded solemnly.

Aunt Sainka spoke up. "I told you, Marusia. I told your brothers! Don't involve yourself in politics! Now look! Your whole family is in danger. They've come to kill you all. They've come to make you all pay."

Marusia's father pulled on his mustache. "We have more food and some money stored in the pit." He looked at Danylo knowingly.

"I'll go back for that," her brother said. "Yosep will come with me."

"And me," Marusia said.

But her father changed his mind. "You both will stay hidden near here. I'll go."

"Rauling will recognize you," Danylo cried.

Father turned on him, face reddening with rage. "You think you're somebody? Some kind of big shot? Your brother did too, and now look what he's caused. You're nothing. You're just a *kulka!*"

Danylo shook his head, widened his stance. "They're not going to look for a little boy, Father. That's exactly it. I'm a little *kulka*, which means I won't bring attention to myself."

Their father glared at Danylo, yanked at his mustache, then threw his hands into the air.

Marusia stepped next to her brother. He was ten. Ten! But he was behaving as if he were twice that age. She was beginning to believe he knew more about the cadre of partisans than she did. But this was what they had been preparing for, wasn't it? This was their fight now.

"I'm going with him," she said.

Danylo groaned and punched Yosep in the arm. "Tell her, won't you? Tell her she can't go."

"They're my friends too," Marusia said.

Yosep sighed. "She's fine. She should come with us."

Marusia looked to her father, but he had retreated to a chair, where he shook his head until it hung low between his shoulders. Marusia went to her weeping mother and hugged her.

"It's time to go," Marusia said soothingly. "The longer we stay in the house, the harder it will be to find a good hiding place."

Danylo and she would wait until the immediate danger had passed, until just before dark.

～

Yosep and Danylo first insisted that they scout out Horodok to find out how many soldiers were left. Afterwards, on the way back to their hideout in the woods, Danylo would head for their farm and dig up their foodstuffs and money. The boys told Marusia to walk far in front of them so that they could keep an eye on her. That was when Marusia remembered Danylo's pistol from that morning. He still had it. This time she felt certain her baby brother was ready to use it.

As soon as the three of them stepped onto the road, they stopped in their tracks. The horizon to the south was alight, the sky dark from thick black smoke.

"They've burned it," Marusia said. "They've burned all the farms. The entire *selo!*"

Yosep pointed toward the smoke. "That's not Uncle Andrij's place. That's your farm."

Marusia thought of her sister, Olia, and turned to the east. There was no fire there either. No smoke that she could see. But other farms were burning in the settlements on the way to Horodok.

Yosep shoved her forward. "We have to get to the church. Before the SS get rid of the bodies."

The three of them reached the village outskirts, but it might as well have been empty. When Marusia had come to visit her friends on warmer evenings—like tonight—she would find the old men smoking their pipes on the streets, catching up with neighbors, or sitting at tables in the front yards, drinking a glass or two. The women would be singing their little ones to sleep, some playing a mandolin. But on this evening, the air was suffocating. Every door and window was shut tight. A lone dog loped along the edges of the shadows, then disappeared, his black fur melting into the dusky shadows. This was not Sheptyk, however. This much she knew. From somewhere inside a barn, sheep and goats cried with neglect.

Marusia realized then that she had not heard a single bell all day. She followed the boys towards the church, its tin onion dome cast in an eerie glow by the fire on the horizon. Yet here, in the village center, there was no fire. Yosep had told them that something more terrible had happened here.

To the right of the priest's home was the graveyard. It was quiet. Nothing there. They moved on to the church. A light spring wind bent the long grass along the edge of the yard, where the children played after school and after the Liturgy. As Marusia approached, the hairs on her arms stood on end at the sight of the dark mounds on the ground.

She halted, and Yosep and Danylo nearly ran into her. They jostled next to one another, Marusia waiting for the boys to go first, but they did not. It was she who had to take the first steps. Mykhailo might be there. He might be amongst them. That got her to move. They needed light. Yosep, thankfully, had a flashlight, and Marusia fell to the ground next to the first corpse. She stifled a sob, her stomach clenching. She recognized Sasha Volykh's mother. Then Sasha's father. In the dim light of Yosep's lamp, Danylo's face looked stricken.

Yosep found Sasha next. Vacant blue eyes stared up into the sky. Marusia moved on, clutching Yosep's collar in her hands and dragging him with her. Silently, without a word, they identified their murdered friends and neighbors. They knew them all. With each new body, Marusia braced herself for Mykhailo's face.

"Marusia, it's the Denehars," Danylo said from the shadows. He'd been friends with Luba's youngest brother. They were the same age.

Now Marusia could no longer hold back the tears. Yosep's hands were shaking as he passed the light over the next two Denehar siblings, and then their father, their mother, and—the last one in the row—Luba. Marusia bit into the heel of her hand and wailed. Danylo dropped down next to Luba's body and gently lifted the bloodied hand away from the face.

The corpse released an unholy scream. "Don't shoot! Mother of God, don't shoot!"

Marusia shrieked. Danylo fell backwards. Yosep dropped the lamp. A light shone suddenly through the school window right across from them. A shadow moved to the door.

"Dear God," Marusia cried. "Luba's alive!" To the shadow in the schoolhouse she cried for help.

Danylo leapt to his feet and ran for the church. He reached for the rope outside the belfry, and rang the bell.

The villagers were jolted into action. The shadow from the schoolhouse materialized into Pan Dmytruk, the schoolteacher. After examining Luba and finding two wounds—one in the shoulder, one in the side—he gently picked her up and carried her to the schoolhouse, Marusia on his heels. He lay her on the table and wordlessly set to work.

Outside, dogs barked and people shuffled out of their homes, lit their lamps, and finally checked for other survivors. But Luba was the only one.

Behind Marusia, a number of the villagers gathered in the doorway of the schoolhouse to watch, talking of miracles in hushed tones.

"The Germans stayed here until sundown, guarding the corpses," Pan Dmytruk said as he reached in with a pair of pliers and removed the first bullet from Luba's shoulder.

Now Marusia understood why nobody had come out earlier to help.

Luba awoke and screeched again. There were murmurs amongst the crowd, and someone came forward with a bottle of spirits and poured it down Luba's throat. Marusia held her down as Pan Dmytruk poured some of it onto Luba's second wound.

Men's voices demanded to be let through into the room. Marusia looked up. People shuffled out of the way, and two men stood before her. She recognized the OUN badges on their forearms.

"You're Lys's sister, aren't you?" one asked Marusia, hardly glancing down at Luba before them.

Marusia shook her head. Who was Lys?

But Danylo shoved in between them. "Yes. And I'm his brother."

"What's your name?" the stranger asked.

"Kulka," Danylo replied.

The stranger smirked. "Kulka?"

For the third time that day, Danylo astonished Marusia.

He puffed out his scrawny chest and said, "That's right. That's my code name. Now, take us to Lys." He looked at her, then back at them. "Take us to our brother."

"You! Child! Come out!"

It was Ruta, hissing down at Marusia between the floorboards. Marusia raised one of the slats, and Ruta helped her with the rest. Their gazes met. Ruta looked wild, her hair uncombed, her blouse untucked. Marusia wondered how she appeared to the woman above, crouched down in the dirt in that narrow, cramped space between the floor and the earth.

"It's not safe here any longer." Ruta's voice was edged with panic.

Marusia did not want to move. It was not Ruta's decision as to when she should move to another safe house, but Ruta was already yanking at the grimy shoulders of Marusia's worn yellow cardigan. When Marusia emerged from beneath the floor, Ruta told her that the Gestapo had rounded up thirty people, shot most, hung the others. This time, in the night. Marusia stared at Ruta. What about Danylo? What about her parents? They were also in a safe house somewhere. But Ruta did not know where.

Marusia had never felt more alone, more vulnerable, but Ruta was busy cursing the Banderites.

"They've provoked this." Ruta paced to the window and back. "They've been setting houses on fire, killing Poles in the settlements. And that disgusts the Germans. Imagine that! Suddenly the German feels all righteous." She spit and glared at Marusia. "What are you looking at me like that for? The Poles, Marusia. Remember? They took our language? Our church? They oppressed us for twenty years."

"I know," Marusia said. Still, she was not certain she would go so far as to kill entire families.

"So you know what the Gestapo does? They say they'll treat us just like we have the Poles. Throwing our children on the fires," Ruta cried. She took in a deep breath, brushed her arm across her mouth. "They're looking for you partisans."

"I'm not a Banderite," Marusia protested.

"Follow Mel'nyk or Bandera—I don't care. Partisans. That's all. Anyone not collaborating with them is an enemy."

"I'll run," Marusia decided. "I have no other choice." How would Lys find her again?

Ruta put an end to the idea. "They've surrounded Ulianyky. You'll have to stay until they're gone, but not in the house."

"Then where?"

Ruta handed her a small shovel and pointed out to the fields beyond the window. "There."

Marusia looked at the shovel, then at the fields. The ground was soaked with moisture, and the farmers had piled up the manure for spreading onto their fields. There were numerous mounds dotting the stubbled ground.

She looked at Ruta, confused, but the woman just nodded

at her. "They wouldn't dare get those fancy uniforms all dirty searching through shit."

Marusia's insides clenched. Who else had to do this? At the same time, she realized how brilliant the idea was.

"I'll come for you at dark, get you out, let you eat and drink something, but you're at great risk in this house."

Ruta was doing what she thought was right, Marusia knew that.

"Get word to Lys," she urged the woman. "Tell him we've been compromised. He must find me a guide and get me out of here." She was certain Mykhailo was busy saving his own skin, but she had nowhere else to turn.

The sun shone brightly in the midmorning sky as Marusia dashed out into the open. On the road she could hear the droning of German vehicles. Her yellow cardigan was now stained and browned after weeks of wear. She tried to launder her clothes at least twice a week, sobbing as she did so, humiliated by the unwashable stink of fear. This was going to be worse. Much worse.

Ducking behind each pile as she went, the sweet, fermented smell of the fertilizer surrounded her. Marusia buried her nose into her arm. The manure was wet from the spring rains, choking the air with hot humidity. It reminded her of the stench of rotten meat, and her stomach churned.

She chose a pile closest to the woods. She moved to avoid being seen from the road and dug the small shovel in. When she heard several motorcycles, she switched to her hands, forming a large enough cave that she could fit into. She crawled in, grabbing what she had shoveled out to patch up the entryway and then patting the manure around her to avoid having bits and pieces falling onto her. When she was finished, she had one small hole through which she could see the trees beyond and allow air in; the air she needed to weep herself to sleep. When she awoke, all was still. Only the wasps and flies continued to drone on.

"Coming!"

Marusia nearly laughed at the sound of Olia's voice behind the door. When her sister finally opened it, Olia's serene face crumpled into a frown.

"What do you want?"

"Olia," Marusia said. She pulled the scarf off her head. "It's me."

Slow recognition dawned on her sister's face. Olia called to the heavens above and opened her arms. Marusia fell into them.

"Look at you," Olia cried as she helped Marusia take off the heavy clothing. She lifted the ends of Marusia's hair, cropped short save for the few curly strands that clung to her damp cheekbones.

Marusia had been fighting the tears since she had spotted the house, her heart exploding at the sight of the farm. She embraced Olia once more and clung to her sister until Olia gently pulled away and led Marusia to the kitchen. Marusia unshouldered her backpack and dropped onto a stool. It had been over half a year since they had last seen each other—a half a year since the Germans had invaded and burned down the Hanchar home.

"How?" Olia said, bringing out a bottle of *horilka* and pouring each of them a shot. "How did you get here?"

It had been a great risk, but Marusia had been sent as a courier to a nearby village, and after her debriefing and delivering the correspondences and documents to the leadership of the local cadre, the close proximity of Horodok made the temptation to visit her family too strong. Her caution had lost this time.

"I have just one day," Marusia said. "One night." She had to meet her escorts in the woods and take the route back to the underground bunker where she was now sheltering. But she could not tell Olia any of this, and Olia did not ask.

Olia prepared a plate of food, and Marusia ate hungrily at first, then paused and slowly brushed the crumbs off from around her. She picked a piece from the loaf and delicately spread a little butter on it.

Olia watched her quietly from her chair at the table. "Where is Mykhailo? We haven't seen him since he came for Danylo."

"You know I can't answer that," Marusia whispered. "I saw him in Boholuba last, though, and we've been in the woods since."

"How many now?"

Speaking about it was not allowed. But this was her sister. Danylo had hid here just a few months ago. Her sister was not stupid. "Maybe fifty of us. Every day, more. Listen, I can't tell you more than that. I'm sorry."

Olia nodded. "The Germans tried to recruit Khoma to fight the Red Army. When they saw his limp, they left him alone. They've taken all of our livestock save for our oldest cow."

"I saw our property," Marusia said. "Nothing left but the well."

"Khoma found bits of charred boxes, but they smashed or took everything else. But no, nothing left." Olia sat back a little and folded her arms. "Did you hear about Gregor's suicide? You partisans are—"

"It's better than being taken alive and tortured," Marusia interrupted. "How does one make a decision about one's friends under torture? We know that if we give anything away, we've compromised our entire cell."

"Does this all not... frighten you?"

Marusia looked down at the hands in her lap. Her fingernails were dirty and crusted. "I would like to believe it would never happen to me. It always happens to someone else. Like Gregor."

They were quiet again. Olia took a slight breath and continued. "Our cousin, Anna, was not allowed to re-enter the gymnasium even though her marks were excellent."

"How is Uncle Andrij and the family?"

"Surviving. We've still got the thrasher hidden, and we grind the wheat at night."

They continued in this matter-of-fact manner, Marusia maintaining that careful distance from her emotions. Just list off the inventory of exploits, wins, tragedies, and losses. It was what made her a good nurse too. But sitting with her sister, a desire to feel vulnerable seeped into her, and Marusia asked herself, had their lives become so primitive that she could no longer allow herself that luxury—to simply feel herself?

She finished the last of her bread and refused any more from Olia. "Later. I'm starving, and I don't want to get sick."

Olia played with the hem of her apron. "You look fine though. I mean, better than I thought you would."

"We *are* fine."

Her sister met her gaze, but hers was sharp, judgmental. "Why are you doing this?"

Marusia shrugged, pretending not to understand the question.

"Is it worth it, I mean?" Olia choked. "Is it worth dying a heroine, dying in the forest? For what?"

"I told you, we're fine."

"The OUN is being hunted because of the reprisals on the Poles."

"Those are Bandera supporters. We follow Mel'nyk."

Olia leaned back and cocked her head. "Really, Marusia? Is there a difference? I mean, really? Tell that to the Jewish families that were deported from the village across the river."

"Yes, there is a difference. We don't punish or torture Ukrainians just because they do not believe in what we do. We don't go to the Polish settlements and nail their children to the tables. We don't hack off people's heads—"

"Stop!" Olia's expression had twisted into a pained grimace. "I know what they do."

"I'm not one of them." Marusia gritted her teeth. "None of us in Lys's group are. I've never turned in a Jew, either. I had nothing to do with any of that."

Olia took in another sharp breath and nodded. "If you say so." She started to say something but hesitated. After a while, she said measuredly, "I know where Mother and Father are."

Marusia crumpled. Her pulse raced, her stomach clenched, and cold sweat beaded across her brow. She barely managed a whisper. "Where?"

"They're in Ulianyky. I don't know with whom, but I know they're there. Khoma knows how to get to them."

Ulianyky. That was where Ruta had hidden Marusia. "But I was almost caught there... Are you sure?"

"Yes," Olia replied. "They've been there all this time. I only learned of it a few days ago."

Marusia gripped the sides of her chair. She had been so close to her parents while hiding at Ruta's. All this time and she had been so close. It was agony, all this secrecy. All this not knowing. She knew why, and she understood that it was for the protection for all those in hiding, but it did not make it any easier. It did not make it any easier either knowing that her sister knew where their parents were hidden. The risk was great even though Olia and her husband were not on the list of the hunted.

That afternoon, Olia's husband returned from the fields, and Olia spoke to him in private, then told Marusia to bundle herself up. Before sunset, Marusia and her sister walked to Ulianyky. They made their way past charred fields and forests, past the rubble of burned-down houses and barns. Autumn had nothing in which to blossom and flash her colors except for the last of the wildflowers that grew along the road. Marusia picked a late daisy and gently put it behind her sister's ear. They smiled a little at each other and continued walking in silence.

Dusk had fallen on Ulianyky by the time they reached the house where Olia believed their parents to be. At the door, a thin woman with graying hair watched them with great suspicion.

Marusia shared the coded message. "We're here to collect some eggs for Father Donenko."

The woman leaned out the doorway a little, rubbed her hands, then gestured for Olia and Marusia to come inside. "Please bear with me a moment. My husband has brought some guests tonight. I'll see to them first and then get those eggs."

Marusia shook her head, confused.

The woman smiled nervously, her voice taking on a lighter tone. "We have some authorities from the protectorate here..."

It was as if the woman had shoved a rock down Marusia's throat.

Olia spoke. "Would you prefer we return another time?"

"No, no," the woman replied, suddenly very accommodating. "Father Donenko must eat tonight, don't you think?"

She led Olia and Marusia into a small room cramped with furniture and lit by candles. Marusia stopped at the couch. The furniture looked familiar. Of course it did. It was her father's handiwork. She stared at the woman, then at the room. More pieces were recognizable. Who were these people? The sound of forks scraping against plates made her skin crawl. Who were the people in the room on the other side of the house?

The woman was all sweetness and politeness now. Obviously she had gathered her wits about her. "Would you young ladies please wait here?"

She drew a curtain over the doorway closest to them and

paused, gave them a meaningful look, and gently tapped on the wall directly next to the doorframe. She smiled sweetly and disappeared behind the curtain.

Olia sat stiffly on the edge of the sofa, but Marusia frowned, looking around the room. She suddenly thought of Danylo and the pistol. If only... She sank down next to her sister.

"If they're here," Olia whispered, "we'll never be able to see them. We should go."

If they were here? "I thought you said they were."

Olia nodded. "They are. But where?" She gestured at the furniture-filled room.

Marusia leapt to her feet and went to the wall, tapping softly so as not to be heard. Nothing was different in the sounds along the wall. It all sounded hollow. She gasped a little. At the curtain, she tried the ends of the thick walls, finding exactly the spot where the woman had tapped. Ruta had had a similar system. The board moved under Marusia's pressure, and Olia was suddenly at her side, her breathing quickening.

"Do you really think..." Olia whispered.

Marusia removed the board and slid it to the side. Olia handed her the candle from a nearby sconce, and they aimed its light inside the wall. Two startled old faces peered back at them, dark eyes half lost in the folds of wearied lids.

Marusia exhaled, and tears swam in her eyes before spilling over. Next to her, Olia covered her mouth to stifle a sob. Marusia's parents blinked back at them, transforming from terror stricken to grief stricken in seconds. Marusia reached to touch them but pulled back at the eruption of laughter on the other side of the house. It was a cruel moment. And it was futile. There was no time to waste.

As she slid the board back into place, she heard the footfalls coming back. She shoved Olia aside and scrambled away from the curtain. Their hostess entered a moment later with a fake smile on her face.

"There you are, ladies," she said, pressing a bundle of wrapped eggs into Marusia's open hands. "Be well, then. May God grant you peace on this night."

The next morning, before dawn, one of Lys's couriers appeared at Olia's door. Marusia got dressed, the courier's only exchange being, "Lys knows. He's not happy."

Marusia hugged her sister tightly, kissed her cheeks, and wiped at the tears on them. She did not know whether they were Olia's tears or hers.

THE PARTISANS: PART THREE
DANYLO

Luts'k, 1943

Danylo was concentrating so hard on putting the last stitch into the silver button of a girl's coat that the pounding on the door sent him flying off his stool.

Filipchuk, a tape measure strung around his neck, looked up from the fabric on the table and laughed. "They don't knock like that."

"I know," Danylo grumbled. He brushed himself off, went to the door, and opened it.

A young man hovered in the street. He wore a brown cap and shifted his gaze from Danylo to the interior of the tailor shop.

"Kulka?" the man asked.

In an instant, Danylo transformed his persona, switched to his nom de guerre. He nodded.

"Good," the stranger said. "Lys wants you to move."

"Why?" Filipchuk asked behind Danylo. "He's safe here."

The courier jerked a thumb over his shoulder. "The area's compromised. The Gestapo recruited Poles to raid every house.

They take anyone remotely suspicious into custody." He shifted his look to Danylo. "Those Poles are exacting a fine revenge, rooting out our partisans."

He told Danylo the location where he would be picked up, asked him to repeat it, then turned away and disappeared around the corner like a feral tomcat.

Danylo knew the location. He had a distant cousin nearby. He wasted no time. In the next room, he stuffed his few possessions into his rucksack and checked to make sure his pistol was loaded before stepping back into the tailor's shop. He stuffed the pistol into his trousers and tightened the string that held them up.

Filipchuk stood between the door and the measuring table, arms crossed over his chest. "You know, I offered to make you a belt."

Danylo smiled and picked up the pink coat he'd been working on. "It's almost finished." He folded it over his chair, then clapped the tailor on the arm. "Thanks, Filipchuk."

As Danylo he would have addressed the man with the respectable "Pan," but he was Kulka now. Kulka was a partisan. Partisans were not beholden to formalities, save with their commanding officers.

"Shame, really," Filipchuk said. "Maybe you'll come back and work for me when the war's over."

Danylo beamed and turned his palms upwards, weighing each option. "Tailor or carpenter? Tailor or carpenter? So many choices available to an ex-partisan."

Filipchuk put a hand on Danylo's shoulder and shook him a little. "Survive first, little Kulka. Then we'll talk about which trade you're best suited for."

Outside of Luts'k, Kulka took the road north and veered off it some ten kilometers outside the city. He was heading into the woods again. Sometime after, he heard grunting and wet chomping sounds. Danylo approached cautiously, hidden by the thick brush. The source of those noises was a pack of wolves pulling and tearing at a deer carcass. One wolf, his teeth bared, looked up and sniffed the air. Danylo touched the pistol at his waist. Eight shots. That's all he had. The wolf lowered its head, and Danylo backed away, making a wide arc around them.

When he reached the location where someone—Lys himself maybe?—should pick him up, all he found were the remains of a small fire. He dropped his rucksack, checked the sky, and realized it had taken him longer than he had calculated. He was late. He considered going to find those cousins of his. Lys would certainly figure it out, would know where to look.

He lay back, removed the apple and the bread from his bag, and ate. He stirred the ashes and decided against relighting the fire. He would wait a little while longer. Just doze a little. His older brother had not disappointed him yet. They'd come for him.

It was the metallic sound of a bridle that awoke him. He opened one eye and saw a black hoof pawing at the dirt. The horse was like the Arabian they'd had at the farm. The animal snorted. Danylo awoke and scrambled to his feet, forgetting he had the pistol in his hand. It dropped to the ground, and he grabbed it, turned it, and pointed it at the horseman. The man was dressed in a black leather coat though it was summer. The long mustache reminded Danylo of his father. The rider studied him and calmed the horse.

"Who are you?" Danylo demanded, wishing his hand would stop shaking.

"I could ask the same, you little scrapper." The man chuckled. It was not a friendly sound. He steered his horse around Danylo. "Where's your family?"

"Dead," Danylo said.

"You Polish?"

"Would I be answering you in Ukrainian if I were?"

The man laughed. "Plenty of them have in the last weeks. Where are you from?"

"Luts'k."

"And you're here to what? Take in some fresh air? Go camping?"

Danylo shook his head, his mind finally cleared. Kulka. He was Kulka, and he was a partisan. It was time he behaved as one. "Maybe you're the Pole."

The man bellowed and slapped his knee. The black horse nickered. The rider showed Danylo the armband around his upper forearm. "You see that? UPA. I'm UPA, and you're on my land—Ukrainian land. Now, I'll ask you again. Who are you?"

"Kulka." Danylo kept his voice steady. "From Luts'k." He was not going to show fear in the face of a Bandera follower.

The man's smile broadened. "Kulka. That you are. All right, if you won't tell me your proper name and where you're from, you'll just come with me. I've got work for anonymous boys like yourself."

The man spurred the horse towards him. Danylo raised the pistol, his finger on the trigger. The Banderite snatched the weapon from his hand. A shot rang into the air. The man wheeled his horse around and swiped Danylo up next, slamming him hard into the saddle. With horror, Danylo watched the countryside speed by.

The men around the bonfire were cocky and self-confident, proclaiming their oaths, calling for a glorious Ukraine, for a glorious battle and death to the enemies. Danylo watched them sullenly from the bench against the house. He could run away, but where to? The entire village seemed to be Banderites, and he really did not know where he was. He'd arrived with the horseman, who called himself Nestor and who'd placed Danylo under the careful watch of three older boys, none of whom warmed to him.

"He's just a baby," one sneered.

"What are we supposed to do with him?" the round-shouldered one asked Nestor. He was four times Danylo's size. "Look at him. What good is he anyway?"

Nestor accepted a bottle of *horilka* from one of his comrades and took a pull before answering. "He's got a pistol, that's what. He's better armed than the lot of you." He cocked his head at Danylo and sucked his teeth. "You any good with it?"

Danylo glared at him. "Better than all of you here."

Nestor grinned widely and swung his arms out to the entire group. "You hear that, boys? We have a sharpshooter here. This little scrapper is going to show us what a great shot he is!"

He strode over and yanked Danylo off the bench, then dragged him to the tied-up horse. He reached into his saddlebag and removed the pistol he'd ripped out of Danylo's hands earlier. He bounced it lightly in his palm.

"Tokarev." Nestor chuckled enviously. "Semiautomatic." He checked the magazine and handed Danylo the weapon. Nestor emptied the bottle and marched to a tree stump at the end of the yard. Kindling was piled up around the trunk.

"All right, little scrapper," Nestor called. "Let's see what you've got."

"You can go a little closer," one of the men prodded.

"He probably doesn't even know where the trigger is," someone else jeered.

Someone tried to shove Danylo forward, but Danylo twisted away and walked backwards. When he was approximately thirty paces from the stump, he raised the pistol and aimed.

Nestor picked up the bottle, eyebrows raised like question marks. "Here, or here," he teased, wiggling the bottle over the stump.

Danylo waited. Nestor released the bottle delicately and stepped away. The other five men and the boys gathered off to the sides.

"He's never going hit that," a man said near Danylo's right shoulder. "You're off, boy. Move to the right."

Danylo held steady. The light was fading. The bottle was clear. He pulled the trigger. The bottle shattered over the stump, and the men and boys broke into a cheer. Someone clapped him on the back.

Danylo faced Nestor when he returned. "Put another one up." He strode back about another dozen steps.

Grinning, Nestor went to scrounge up another empty bottle. The man who had stood behind Danylo exclaimed for a second time that his aim had been off. The other men laughed and jostled one another, saying obviously the aim had been spot on.

"A natural," someone called.

Yosep had called Danylo that too. When they'd discovered the cache at the Bolshevik bunker, Danylo and his cousin had loaded a rifle, and by the third day, Danylo was shooting bull's-eyes on the targets they'd chalked onto tree stumps, sixty paces away.

Nestor finally found and placed another bottle on the stump. The sun was dropping behind the trees. Danylo took aim once more and pulled the trigger. At the sound of glass breaking, he stuffed the pistol into his waist and stalked back to sit on the bench. The pistol would not leave his possession again.

The men hurried to the stump to check the damage. The boys demanded to have a look at Danylo's pistol. They quieted down when Nestor returned, sucking on his teeth again.

"This one here says your aim was off," Nestor said, indicating the man who had been standing behind Danylo. He grinned and laughed. "He swears it."

The man who'd doubted Danylo's aim nodded.

Danylo shrugged. "It's my pistol. I know how to aim it."

The men around him laughed. The boys asked again to have a try with the weapon, the biggest stating he had rights, after all, because he was Nestor's son.

"Leave him be, Zenko," Nestor said. "The pistol belongs to him. Kulka, you said? Yeah, see, you boys couldn't shoot a pumpkin in a patch. Besides"—he scratched his head—"we don't steal from one of ours, right, Kulka?"

Danylo held his gaze.

Nestor glanced over his shoulder at the men around him.

"So, Kulka," Nestor said, scratching his chest beneath the leather coat, "you know how to ride a horse?"

The roan dropped its head and foraged the forest floor as Kulka slipped off its back and crawled to the edge of the tree line. Crouched in the brush, he was facing a field of cut wheat and another area of forest beyond that. The sun was setting to his right, and it lit up the small Polish settlement at the end of the field to the east. Two German trucks and three motorcycles were parked in front of the largest building. A few older men were leaning on the wall of the building, caps pulled down against the glare of the sunset.

Kulka noted movement in the trees across from him. That burly Zenko was worthless in hiding! Kulka waved his hand downwards, and Zenko grimaced, made an obscene gesture, but moved back into the trees on his side of the woods. When he was hidden again, Kulka returned his gaze toward the village.

Two men in German uniforms stepped out, one unfolding a sheet of paper, the other heading straight for one of the vehicles. The Polish men pushed themselves away from the wall and went to the trucks. They began loading containers into them.

The man with the document blew a whistle, and several soldiers appeared from various areas of the village.

This was it. This was what they were here for, he and Nestor's boys. Kulka's heart raced, and he gripped his pistol tighter. They were here to rattle the Germans' nerves. And the Poles'. This was for Ukraine. It was not so different to what Lys and the members of his *sotnia* were doing except that here, Kulka was no longer simply a boy in hiding. Here, he no longer simply distributed papers. He was in the action now.

The signal was a sparrow call. Kulka raised his weapon into the air, called one time, received a response—two, three—and crouched down in the brush. He pulled the trigger and emptied the cartridge, smiling as the men in the village dashed and took cover, the Germans clamping down their helmets over their heads.

Kulka refilled the magazine—his last one, so he'd have to make it count. Nestor certainly had more. He swung back into the saddle of the roan and cantered through the forest as Kulka fired eight more rounds. On the other side of the woods, the boys were throwing the hand grenades. The field exploded to Kulka's right. His horse whinnied, picked up speed, and Kulka wheeled the animal back to where he'd come from. Shots were fired. Shouts came from the settlement. The boys in the woods moved. Kulka urged the horse into a gallop. Engines revved in the distance behind him. They were sending the Nazis on a wild-goose chase. That was all they were supposed to do, so when he saw Zenko come out into the open field, Kulka yanked on the reins, pulled his horse up, and swung it around.

What was that dimwit up to? Did Zenko think he was a Cossack horseman? As they had ridden out of Nestor's *selo*, the huge boy, his long blond hair bouncing beneath the cap, had barely gotten his animal to trot before he'd begun losing his balance.

Now Zenko's horse was at a gallop and Zenko was swinging

his cap in the air, shouting, "Glory to Ukraine! Glory to the heroes!" Zenko's huge frame suddenly tilted sideways in the saddle, and his feet came up behind him. In the next instant, Zenko was on the ground, the horse racing for home.

Kulka kicked his own horse forward and was about to charge out of the woods, when Zenko stood and hobbled through the dried cuttings. Kulka looked to the east. The Germans' vehicles were gone, but two of the Poles stood in wide stances at the end of the field. They held rifles, and they were aiming straight at Zenko.

It was only supposed to be a joke. It was not a battle.

"Get down, you idiot," Kulka shouted.

Zenko turned to him with that indignant glare again. In the next moment, a rifle shot, and Zenko flailed, as if he were trying to shake something off his arm. He twisted his body towards the village, and Kulka saw the look of disbelief. Another shot. Half of Zenko's forehead flew into the air.

Kulka yanked the reins and spurred his horse back through the woods, back to Nestor's *selo*, back to the Banderites.

"What's happened?" Nestor demanded when Kulka stumbled into the house.

The Banderites were sitting around a table, a lamp placed in the middle of strewn-about maps.

"Zenko," Kulka said.

Nestor tipped his head. "My Zenko?"

Kulka nodded. He swallowed. *Get it out. Only report.* "He got shot. He's dead."

Nestor rose and strode out the door, the other men following him. Kulka fell in with them and watched as Nestor ran down the road. The two other boys were coming in on their ponies, their eyes wild.

"Zhenia! Tolia," Nestor shouted. "Where's your brother?"

The boys leapt from their mounts, sobbing, choking out the news. Someone held a lamp up.

Nestor turned, his face twisted with rage. He yanked at his mustache. His glare landed on Kulka. "You," he growled. "Get back to your horse. You're taking us to him."

The other men did not need further instructions. By the time Kulka had drunk and given his horse some water and was back in the saddle, the other men had gathered around, torches held up in the early-fall twilight. Kulka saw that some held axes, another a hoe, and someone else a spade. Another man hooked a long rope to his saddle.

Nestor rode up next to Kulka. "Give me your pistol."

Kulka shook his head.

Nestor leaned dangerously in his saddle. "Give me the pistol."

Kulka slowly reached into his trousers, past the string that held them up, and withdrew the gun. He laid it into Nestor's hand.

"How many rounds did you shoot?"

"All of them."

Nestor made a gesture. "Give me the ammunition."

Kulka swallowed, but when he spoke, his voice was hoarse. "I don't have any more."

Nestor growled, spit at the ground, and tossed the pistol into the dirt after it. He steered his horse in the direction of the Polish settlement. The others followed him. Kulka jumped off his horse and retrieved the pistol, relieved they were leaving him behind.

"Not so fast," one man said, returning. He held his torch above Kulka's head. It was the man who had doubted his aim the night before. "Get back on the horse. You heard Nestor. You're coming with us."

The ride back to the village was too short. Kulka moved up ahead and passed Nestor without looking at him. He retraced his steps in the woods that had earlier hidden him. In the dark, he saw the winking lights through the trees. The Polish settlement. A bonfire burned in front of the largest building. People moved about the yard and around the fire. He heard voices speaking Polish.

Kulka stopped his horse, nervous about being seen with the torches. This was no longer going to be about pranks and jokes.

In the dark, Nestor said. "Where is he?"

Kulka pointed to the field. "Somewhere around here, in that field there. That's where it happened."

Nestor told the men to put the flames out. Then he turned to Kulka and demanded he show him exactly where. They walked through the field in the dark. In the village, a dog barked, but Nestor did not slow down. He was scanning the ground, bent at the waist, looking for Zenko's corpse.

They found nothing. Kulka measured the distance between the village road and where they were now. They were too close. Now, more dogs barked.

"He's not here," he whispered.

Nestor stalked back to the group waiting in the woods. "They took the body. Those bastards are celebrating my son's death."

Nobody said anything. A horse nickered. Finally, Nestor said, "We wait. Then we go get him. And those sons of whores."

It had to be long past midnight when the last light went out, and Kulka shivered in the brush. The season was changing, and the nights had grown colder, the ground damp with frost. Nestor moved a little next to him, and Kulka raised his head.

"Now," Nestor said. "We go now."

There was a sound, like a sickle dragging along the grass. Kulka saw the gleam of a knife in the Banderite leader's hand. Someone returned with canisters, and Kulka thought he smelled kerosene. The other tools—the axes, the hoe, the rope—they, too, reappeared. These were their weapons, Kulka realized. And he did not have anything other than an empty pistol. He started to turn around, but someone in the group grabbed hold of his collar and pushed him forward. The Banderites crouched and crawled through the woods, edging closer and closer to the village.

"Glory to Ukraine," someone whispered near Kulka. "Glory to our heroes."

They had reached the road between the field and the village. Kulka followed the bent figures to the bonfire, where the last embers still glowed. He smelled kerosene and the torches, and the bonfire flamed anew. The shadows of the Banderites moved in a quiet line. Now in the village, Kulka could make out that there were about a half dozen houses altogether. Three men moved to the first house on the far left. Three others to the one on the right. He heard liquid splash, saw the torches lowered, and the doorways of the two houses were alight. Quickly, the two groups moved to the next homes. Kulka waited in the middle, near the bonfire.

Nestor strode over to him, baring his teeth. "You." He shoved Kulka in front of the largest house. "When they come out, you just aim."

But the pistol is empty, Kulka wanted to remind him. He was defenseless, useless.

The shouts inside the houses—four were now burning—transformed from surprise to horror then to outrage. Kulka saw the door to a house on his right open, and a woman stepped back, arm up, screaming as the flames licked towards her face. Hot, thick smoke was choking him too. Shadows moved around the sides of the houses. He heard more screams; another house was lit. He heard heavy thuds landing on soft objects, wet sounds, and shouts of terror.

When he blinked and faced the middle house again, a woman, a man, and two young girls stood before Kulka, uncertain, looking beyond him, edging towards him. He raised his pistol, cocked it, and held it steady.

They stopped before Kulka, and the man raised his hands, his face drawn tight.

"What do you want with us here?" he asked in Ukrainian. "We're Ukrainians."

Out of the dark, Kulka saw the gleam of something metallic and sharp come heavily down on the man's head. He crumpled beneath the sickening crunch. Something splattered onto Kulka's face. He took a step back. The children turned, voiceless. Just like him. The woman screamed. Two figures in black moved to either side of her, and one drove something through her middle. She doubled over, her cry cut down to a stifled groan. The pitchfork. Kulka lowered his pistol just as the two Banderites swiped up the children. Now the girls screamed. They kicked and fought as the men swung them back to their burning home. The children flew through the open door, back into the inferno.

Kulka whirled away, but Nestor approached him again. He stepped into the ring of light and wiped his knife in the grass. In his other hand, he held something up. The hair. A face. The head.

Kulka turned to the darkness behind him. He ran.

A rooster crowed, and Kulka curled himself tighter into the hay, his teeth still chattering. Every muscle was stretched and cramped, and he ached all over. He burrowed deeper into the sweet-smelling grass, and still he could not stop shivering. Reprieve came in the sound of a door opening. He lifted his head and crawled far enough out to look into the farmyard. He recognized his cousin right away. He'd found her. He scrambled out of the haystack and climbed down the ladder before Havka could come into the stable.

She stopped in the doorway just as he reached the bottom rung. "Who are you?"

"Havka, it's me," Kulka said, turning to face her. "Danylo Hanchar, Ivan's son."

She rushed to him. Smiling, she turned him around. "Danylo, my goodness you've grown!" She sounded relieved. "Mykhailo was looking for you a couple of days ago. He's worried sick about you."

"Where are they?"

"They've had to move to Polissia," she said. "The Germans' retaliations have put them in grave danger."

Kulka's heart sank. Lys was somewhere in that vast forest, which stretched to the borders of Belarus and Poland.

"Where have you been?" Havka steered him towards a stall. Only one cow was in the whole barn. She grabbed a bucket and moved her hands beneath the udder. Milk squirted into the pail. She looked up. "You look hungry. Are you all right?"

Kulka wondered how to answer all her questions.

"Anyway," she said, "Mykhailo told me how to get word to him. And then he said he's got a job for you. Back in Luts'k."

"But I just came from there," he complained, though he did miss Filipchuk and those bulletins.

Havka pulled the pail out and took a tin cup hanging from the wall. She dipped it into the pail and handed it to him. He drank. She filled the cup twice more, then wiped her hands on her apron.

"I don't know anything about that, but he wants you to go back and do something for them. My husband will accompany you."

Kulka shook his head, the milk filling his stomach. He wanted to just sleep. That was all. He shivered and sniffed. Angrily, he brushed away a tear.

Havka pursed her lips and pulled him to her. "Come now, Danylo. Come with me into the house. You get some rest first."

She led him through the yard but stopped before going into the house. From a wicker basket, she removed a large cloth with red-and-white embroidery. A tablecloth. She patted Kulka's shoulder and carried it to the wash line and hung it. When she returned, she ran a hand over his head.

"Now they know you're here."

Kulka slept deeply beneath the down covers. When he awoke, it was dark outside, and it had turned unseasonably warm again. Crickets chirped in the tall grasses before the forest. He went into the kitchen and stopped in the doorway.

A man was seated at the table, noisily sucking the meat out of a pig's ear. He dropped it into his bowl and rose.

Havka stopped washing the plate she had in her hand and nudged the man. "This is my husband," she said. "Viktor."

"Come here." Viktor waved Kulka in. "Come. Sit and eat." He grabbed a bowl from the middle of the table and ladled tripe soup into it. Then he lifted the bottle of *horilka* next to him and poured Kulka a small amount into a glass. Havka poured a mug of water out of a pitcher and placed it before Kulka and sat down next to him.

They ate, and Kulka looked around the small kitchen. It was dimly lit and warm, and the stew felt good in his belly. When Viktor raised his glass, Kulka did as well and gulped the shot. He shivered a little and wiped his mouth with the back of his hand.

"What is that?" He pointed to a number of jars lined up on a table near the door. They looked like pickled vegetables, but it was hard to discern what exactly was inside.

Viktor twisted in his seat and then, mouth still smacking, smiled and chuckled. Havka made a face and rolled her eyes.

"That there," Viktor said, "are bottles of formaldehyde with specimens. Some of the university buildings in Luts'k were bombed last week. Those are my little treasures."

"His new hobby," Havka said and smiled into her hand.

Viktor was finished with the pig's ear and now helped himself to soup. He pointed the ladle at Havka. "My hobby, sweetheart, is going to put meat on this table all winter long."

Kulka frowned at the funny jars of liquids and solids. "What are you planning to do with formaldehyde?"

Viktor paused in his ladling and grinned again. "Cognac."

"Cognac?"

"That's correct. I'm going to distill cognac for our protectorate."

Now Kulka sat up. "How?"

Viktor jerked a chin at Havka. "Go on. Show him."

Havka rose, looking pleased with herself. She shoved a cupboard a little to the side, then reached behind it and withdrew a sack and held it up for Kulka to read. Sugar.

"Lots of sugar." Viktor laughed. "They'll think we're French by the time we're done with them."

Kulka looked at the sack of sugar, then the bottles of specimens on the table, then—in turn—at Viktor and his cousin. He grinned. Tailor. Carpenter. Distiller. "Can you teach me how?"

Viktor winked, reached over the table, and ruffled Kulka's hair. "I can teach you how. And when we're done in Luts'k, you can make your own batch." His smile dissipated. "Before we go there, you tell me where you've been."

He reached for the bottle of *horilka* and poured some more into Kulka's glass and then into his own. Kulka clamped his mouth shut. He couldn't tell him. The things that he had seen, those men who had sworn allegiance to a free Ukraine, had sworn to eliminate all enemy collaborators... He'd run away too. Glory to the heroes. He was no hero. He'd wanted to be one, but when Nestor...

He squeezed his eyes tight. A hand held his shoulder, and he stiffened. It was Havka. She pulled him to her once more, and for the second time that day, he fought the tears.

She patted Kulka lightly. "I'll leave you two alone. You can talk." She smiled sadly at Kulka. "Man to man."

It took him a while, and by the time Kulka finally told Viktor the bits that he could, Viktor had set up the kitchen to work on the "cognac." Outside, the evening was calm. The war seemed so very far away. At that moment Kulka wondered how that could be. It helped. It helped to put the necessary distance between him and the events with Nestor's men.

As the evening wore on and he learned how to distill the chemicals, Kulka told Viktor everything. Viktor listened, interrupting only to show Kulka the next step in the process.

When Kulka was finished, Viktor put a fatherly arm around him. "That's it then. It's a good thing you found us." Tomorrow, he told Kulka, they would go to Luts'k. "We've got weapons to smuggle out of the city and to Lys's men." He looked Kulka up and down. "We can't get them out, but you can."

Kulka stood under the awning of the Luts'k library, its Greek-styled facade strange to him because it was one of the last whole buildings in the city. His head was drenched, but the rest of him was dry beneath the oversized trench coat. It would do the trick. He shook the rain from his hair and took in the bustling market crowd. The people at the market were scrambling to trade for whatever scraps they could. The train station loomed in the background of the market pavilion. The church that flanked the entryway to the east had a gaping wound. Smoke rose from the contents still smoldering inside. He checked the streets once more, then stepped into the library. He'd been here many times before to deliver the bulletins and flyers he and Filipchuk had produced.

The main reading room was on the second level. In the silence, he realized he was stepping extra carefully, to not make any noise, but the hem of his trench coat whispered along the marbled floor. He approached the main desk. The woman behind it looked up from the book she was reading, smiled absentmindedly, then looked again.

"You," she said, just a hint of a smile.

He only knew her as the Librarian.

Kulka nodded and spoke the password. She inserted a piece of paper in the book, closed it, and rose. Nobody else was in the room that he could see. He followed her back down the stairs and to the area with all the offices. Her heels clicked and echoed along the corridor. Kulka admired her figure as she walked before him. She was in her twenties, slim, with dark lashes framed around intelligent brown eyes. She had a no-nonsense practical manner. And she was brave. Nobody—especially her —would ever know how he felt about her.

She stopped at one door and opened it. The Director, a man with thin whitened hair brushed over his balding head, looked up and removed his dark-rimmed spectacles. The Librarian nodded to the Director as she passed his desk. She fished out a key that hung between her blouse and her chest, and pulled the chain off over her head. She unlocked the door, the older gentleman now standing with them, and all three went inside.

Kulka saw crates, some with their lids removed and books inside. The gentleman wasted no time and retrieved one of those crates. Both he and the Librarian removed four layers of books, stacked thickly. Below that was the bottom of the crate. Kulka glanced at them nervously as they stepped back. Where were the weapons? The ammunition?

The Director smiled and lifted the wooden bottom with a flourish. Beneath a thin layer of straw lay six rifles, hand grenades, and ammunition. Kulka grinned and undid the trench coat.

"Give me the first two and a couple of grenades," he said.

The Director snorted. "You want to carry them out just like

this? I thought you were coming with others." He passed a hand over the storage room. "There's at least fifteen, maybe twenty more boxes like this."

Kulka dropped his arms, but the Librarian stepped in front of him and yanked the trench coat open, frowning.

"This won't do," she said.

Kulka glanced down at the coat. Of course it would. That was the plan. It would hide anything that was bulky.

She was shaking her head, her brow furrowed, and he knew any argument was futile.

The Director was irritated. "You'd have to come back a hundred times. The checkpoint guards will suspect you by that point."

"There are no others," Kulka said. "There's only me."

The Librarian stalked out of the storage room, and Kulka watched her go.

He faced the Director again and shrugged. "I guess we're going to have to do the best we can."

The woman returned, on a mission of her own, apparently. She laid down a pair of scissors, a box of needles, little metal "Os," and a spool of thread. Unceremoniously, she yanked the trench coat off Kulka's shoulders and laid it out on a shelf. She proceeded to rip the seams off the lining, first on one side, then the other. The Director stepped out of the storage room, explaining he would keep an eye on things in the building.

Kulka was alone with the Librarian, and she was alone with her work. He watched over her shoulder as she sewed in the little "Os." She measured the rifles with her eye, then sewed another row of "Os." It felt like an eternity before she was finally finished. Kulka backed away and gave her room as she shook the coat out.

"Good," she said, eyeing the destroyed inside.

"Good?" Kulka said. The lining was hanging in rags. "If they open my coat—"

"I'll stitch up the lining, but only provisionally. We'll have to rip it open each time you come." She held the coat open to him. "Go on. Put it on."

The Director returned just as she was finishing up those provisionary stitches along the edges of his coat. Kulka enjoyed every moment she stood close to him. The older man looked at her, then at Kulka, then back at her.

Kulka grinned and patted the coat's sides. "They're in here, between the leather and lining."

The Librarian had "hung" the rifles in the coat through those little "Os" and hooked all the grenades and ammunition in between. Like this, he would need a week, maybe two, with several trips each day.

The Director sniffed with appreciation, and the Librarian smiled back at the older man in a way that Kulka suspected was more than just friendly camaraderie.

He shrugged. "I guess I'll be back later. An hour or two."

They escorted him to the main doors. Kulka stepped outside, and the Director grabbed his shoulder and jerked his chin towards the pavilion across the road.

"Don't look now. Patrols. I want you to take a different way each time. Understand?"

Kulka nodded, shook the man's hand, then the Librarian's.

She smiled at him and stroked his cheek. "Glory to the heroes."

Kulka took in a sharp breath, tried to smile, and saluted her instead. He descended into the crowd. At the intersection, he turned right and passed the small square used for German parades. The faceless hotel had become the headquarters of the *Reichskanzlei*, where Commander Rauling and his gang directed all their orders. Kulka went down the hill, then headed east to the river. He crossed the bridge without anyone paying any attention to him. The whole charade was easy, but he had learned long ago to never let down his guard.

Viktor waited for him in the woods with the hay wagon. When Kulka arrived, they split the seams and hid the weapons under the hay. Kulka handed Viktor a spool of thread and needle and spread his arms.

Viktor laughed. "You don't actually believe I know how to do that, do you?"

Kulka shrugged. "Learn."

Viktor stopped laughing.

Two weeks later, Kulka had two more trips to make. He begged the Director and the Librarian to let him take it all in one last run.

"They haven't been checking anyone at all today," he insisted.

The Director agreed, seemingly glad the whole ordeal was over. He handed him the last two pistols, some more ammunition, and the last two grenades. Kulka stuffed them all into his pockets. The Librarian frowned.

"You're too bulky." She patted the coat. "You'll draw attention to yourself."

But the Director hurried him out to the corridor.

As Kulka headed for the bridge and checkpoint at the River Stir, he saw that every pedestrian was being manhandled, their coats and bags and rucksacks inspected. He turned around. He had to find a different way out of the city. A line of Wehrmacht soldiers approached the crowd from behind, often checking those on foot but also looking into wagons.

Kulka ducked into the crowd where the carts and wagons were lining up. A car honked. He spun around. A motorcade was trying to push through. More honking. Wagons moved and people shuffled aside. Kulka was standing next to a cart filled with potatoes, and he halted. One of the sedans was slowly pushing its way through the bottleneck, and Kulka recognized Rauling in the back seat. Rauling was the reason he was here now.

He put a hand over one of his pockets. There they were. Two grenades. He could do it. He could do it and probably still manage to get away with it. He looked over his shoulder, over the bridge, and into the river below.

"Psst!"

Kulka jumped.

The old woman with the potato cart jerked her head. "Get in."

The sedan rolled by now, both sides of the road crammed with those who had gotten out of the way. She did not have to invite him a second time. Kulka climbed into the cart and leaned against a sack of potatoes. He grabbed a piece of straw and stuck it between his teeth just as she picked up the handles and headed for the bridge. The patrols were trying to bring order back, and Kulka held his breath as they waved her over. Without hardly anything other than another cursory glance, they waved the woman and Kulka through.

He could have whooped when they reached the end of the bridge. Once they were out of sight, he jumped down. "Thank you."

Her chin bobbed at him, and she nodded before moving on.

When he found Viktor, Kulka opened his arms, laughing. "We're finished." He stroked the horse and jumped into the wagon. There was no need to rip out any seams.

Viktor looked over his shoulder at Kulka. "Polissia?"

Kulka nodded. It was time to meet his brother and the *sotnia*. A reunion was long past due.

He received a hero's welcome, just as he ought to have. Kulka braced himself for the congratulatory claps and shakes from the men in the *sotnia*. Several thanked him over and over as Viktor revealed the cache of weapons. Twenty Mosin Nagant rifles, over three dozen pistols and revolvers, hand grenades, more explosives, and loads of ammunition. Thanks to Kulka, about half the men in the *sotnia* had new weapons, and everyone had plenty of ammunition.

Kulka reached into a separate crate and withdrew two bottles of the distilled spirits he and Viktor had made. The men whooped, but Kulka pressed the bottles to his chest.

"You don't want to be drinking this," he said.

Viktor winked at him and got back to uncovering the cache of weapons.

"Then what should we do with them?" one of the men asked. He followed Kulka to the dugout, where the men said his older brother waited.

Kulka smiled broadly. "Pay off the protectorate. Have them drink it."

Mykhailo stepped out before Kulka had reached the lean-to entrance. He was thin and grim-faced. He looked aged. Kulka dropped his smile. He pressed the two bottles into the hands of a man to his right and went to his brother.

"Lys," Kulka said. He spread his arms out—the way he had seen Nestor do, the way Filipchuk had done to members of the cadre, the way Viktor and he had embraced—a greeting amongst brothers. Mykhailo stepped forward and raised his hand.

The slap landed on Kulka's face so hard that he thought his head would spin off his neck. Kulka covered his face but saw his brother raise his hand again. He tried to backpedal, but he was too late. Mykhailo came after him.

"Bandera's men?" Mykhailo said, his voice hard and cold. Controlled. "You left us to run with a bunch of Banderites?"

Kulka raised his arm again, but the next impact knocked him off his feet. He scrambled up and, doubled over, then charged Mykhailo. Mykhailo held him off, but then he lost his balance. They fell backwards, and there was a terrible crash as the lean-to around the dugout collapsed. Men yanked at Kulka's collar, at his trench coat—the coat that provided these partisans all the weapons they needed—and Kulka swung and kicked blindly. He hit something or someone a few times, but mostly he managed to find air.

Finally a succession of voices. "All right," they muttered. "That does it. That's it, boys. Stop already."

Kulka was released, and he huffed as he watched one of the other officers help Mykhailo to his feet.

Mykhailo stood and brushed himself off with irritated motions before looking up at Kulka again. "When the hell did you grow up?"

Kulka rubbed his face and spit the blood out of his mouth.

Someone laughed and put an arm around him.

But Mykhailo raised a finger. "God will be your judge, boy! And before he gets to you, let me tell you one thing: If I *ever* hear of you running around with those bastards again..." He coughed. "I swear to God I will avenge those families you murdered myself. That's fratricide, what you did. You hear me?"

Kulka straightened, shaking off the arm. "I didn't kill anyone. No one, you hear? And where were you? Huh? Where were you? I was kidnapped by that band, and nobody came to find me." Tears sprang and he hated himself. He stepped back and pointed at his brother. "Don't you lecture me about fratricide. Look at that German uniform of yours!"

Mykhailo stared at him, retrieved a handkerchief from his pocket, and wiped his face. When he was finished, he waved a dismissive hand. "Get him out of here."

"Lys," someone protested. "He's just a boy."

It was too much. Kulka turned and ran. He would run all the way back to Horodok if he had to, but his brother's voice followed him and hands grabbed him. He was returned to stand before Mykhailo again, and the destroyed lean-to of the dugout.

Mykhailo scrutinized him. "Where are the weapons?"

Sulkily, Kulka led him to Viktor's wagon, where Mykhailo inspected the cache.

"I hear you're quite the shot," he said and picked up a revolver.

Kulka scowled. "Who told you?"

"I have someone who's switched sides." He gestured to the growing crowd around the wagon. Kulka's eyes widened when he recognized one of Nestor's men, the one who had discredited Kulka's aim the night he'd shot the bottles.

Kulka turned away and leaned on the wagon. "What's he doing here?"

Mykhailo looked up from a rifle he was holding, one of the Mosin Nagants. "We're all brothers in the end."

He held the rifle towards Kulka. "Go on. Take it. You deserve it."

Kulka eyed him suspiciously. Mykhailo nodded. Kulka took the rifle into his hands.

"Ostep will teach you how to shoot."

"I don't need anyone to teach me how to shoot."

Mykhailo put a hand on his shoulder. "Where we're going, you will."

"Where are we going?"

"Poland. And then who knows after that. Our sister will be joining us."

"Marusia?"

Mykhailo nodded. "She and a few others have taken up nursing duties."

Kulka sniffed and looked down at the dirt. He missed his family. He did not want to ask about his parents. Not just yet. When he faced Mykhailo again, his brother was studying him. He stepped forward and took Kulka into an embrace. Kulka fell into it. For a moment—for as long as the embrace lasted—he was simply Danylo.

Mykhailo pulled away. "All right, Kulka?"

"All right, Lys."

His brother put an arm around him and led him back to the dugout. "Filipchuk says he wants to have you back after the war, make you into a tailor."

Kulka laughed a little. "Yeah, there's a pink coat he wants me to finish for a little girl."

Lys plucked one of the bottles of alcohol from the man who still held them and examined it. He pulled the stopper out with his teeth, spit it out, and took a swig. Kulka watched as he swallowed. Lys smiled broadly. Viktor laughed.

"I don't know." Lys handed Kulka the bottle. "If you're not the sharpshooter they say you are, I think you've got a future in this."

FROM BEFORE TO AFTER-AFTER
WILHELMSHAGEN (BERLIN), 1945

It was washing day and Lida dreaded washing day, but when the guards came to the children's barracks there was nothing she could do. She and the other children marched out to the cement basins, took the sliver of soap and made sure to wash their faces, behind their ears, their hands, their feet, everything. Washing day meant that, afterwards, even the youngest children had to line up and stand still while a stream of people came to look at them. These people chose which of the children to take. Some of the children returned, like Lida, after working all day or maybe more days. She had helped with a harvest, had milked goats, had scrubbed floors, and had pieced together bullets and ammunition. She had made bullets many times. But some of the children never returned. Those with the prettiest hair and the prettiest eyes—the ones that women in furry coats and men in nice hats took the greatest interest in—rarely returned. It was that idea—of never returning, of never seeing her mother again, of Matusia vanishing like Lida's father had done when they'd arrived at the camp—that petrified Lida on washing day. To make her move, to make her feet unstick from the floor, she made herself go to Before.

Before was the world Lida had lived in before her family had been loaded onto those trucks. Before was the place where she had been with her Matusia, with her Bat'ko, safe and sound in Kiev. In Before, being a Communist was good. In After, it was not.

Her mother had been different in Before. Matusia used to dote on Lida and teach her things like how to walk straight, how important dressing properly was, and how to brush her hair. Lida could remember laughing. Her father would come home from work in a large black car and, after millions of kisses, he would take Lida and Matusia for rides around Kyiv. Before was a perfect world.

After was the time from when they arrived at the camp. After was a terrible place, where a father could simply disappear in a crowd of people. Lida was standing at a table with Matusia. Matusia was telling them their names and getting clothing and numbers, and suddenly Bat'ko was gone. That's how Lida remembered it. Vanished into thin air, like the coin a magician she once saw in Kyiv Park made disappear from his hand.

In After, Lida no longer had a father. She still had a mother but Matusia was never *really* there. Matusia was always tired. And she was skinny. And short-tempered with Lida. And she cried a lot. Matusia came back to the bunker late at night and left at dawn. Lida was almost always still asleep then because she lay awake most of the night. She itched everywhere. She was hungry—not just hungry but really-really hungry. Her clothes stank and they were ugly. Everything was gray. And Matusia did not seem to care. She would tell Lida to stop complaining, to eat the food she received, to pool the food together and give some of hers to the smallest and weakest children.

Once, when a new family arrived, Lida made a new friend. There was a mother and her two sons, and the boys' aunt. They said they were from L'viv. They talked differently but Matusia said the family was also Ukrainian. Lida asked the older boy, Yurko, whether his father had come with them, too. She always asked the new children. Did he remember seeing their father after they had spoken to the people at the tables? Yurko had nodded.

"Do you know where he is now?" she asked.

Yurko shook his head, and then he looked scared when Lida told him about her *bat'ko* vanishing at the snap of her fingers. That's what happened in the world of After, she explained. Yurko's mother came and asked what was wrong, why was her son crying? Lida did not want to get into trouble but Yurko asked his mother about his father.

"He's with the other men in the camp," his mother said. She put a hand beneath Lida's chin and said, "His father is here. He's working."

Which meant that perhaps Bat'ko was also working in After. Then he must also be making bullets or collecting hay. If Yurko's mother was so certain he would see his father again, then Lida was certain she would see hers.

Lida decided that Yurko would be her very best friend. But very soon Yurko fell ill. He was very-very sick. His body became skinny, and his head too large, and then his stomach swelled. Yurko's mother and his aunt cried a lot, like Matusia, and they rocked him, and everyone put together food for him like potatoes, even with the rotten parts, the bits of bread, some of that rain-puddle soup.

One woman said, "Don't give him any more. He's retaining water. His heart will drown."

Lida tried to picture that, tried to understand how a heart could drown in her body. Matusia said, "Imagine sadness is like water." And Lida could imagine a heart drowning in sadness. She really could.

Then one morning, Lida woke up to hushed voices and she

sat up in the bed where she lay next to Matusia and she saw that Yurko's mother and his aunt were standing over him but what was more amazing was that there was a man in the barrack and he was not in uniform. He was thin and he was hunched over a little even when he stood straight. Because when he stood straight, he had Yurko in his arms and he told the women—in their funny Ukrainian—to get Yurko's brother dressed. They were going to the doctor.

Lida had slid out of her bed and she followed them to the door. She watched the man and the women and the little boy march to the entrance of the camp. The man with the funny bump on his back was carrying Yurko in his arms. There were words. More soldiers joined the group. Lida heard the man yell, "You need my sons to fight for your Hitler. Is this how you plan to win the war? By killing all the boys?"

The man was Yurko's father!

Lida squatted at the corner of the nearest bunker and watched. The family was told to stand off to the side. The patrol lifted a phone in the box. Lida waited. Another man came. He wore a black hat. He was the one everyone listened to. He talked to Yurko's father, and he talked to Yurko's mother, then to the aunt, and there were hands moving and Yurko's head rolling back in his father's arms. Then something even more magical happened. The man that everyone listened to gave Yurko's father a piece of paper, then he waved at the soldiers and the soldiers walked to the gate, opened it then—

Lida shook her head now. She put the sliver of soap into the water. She laughed into her hand. The guard across from her looked at her funny, made his gun point at the cement basin. She scrubbed at her ears.

Then, she continued telling herself, *Yurko's family walked into the world of Before.*

"Do you have any nice dreams, Lida?" Jacek asked her.

Lida pushed the finished tray of bullets aside. Her fingers tingled. A boy she did not know collected the trays. She waited until he was gone. "I sometimes dream about my father," she said.

"I don't remember mine," Jacek said.

It was the start of the conversation every time. It was Jacek and Marina and Katia asking Lida to tell a story, *the* story.

"Once," she started, "I was really sick and my parents sent me to my aunt's in the Crimea. When I was better, my aunt wrote a letter to tell them but when the letter arrived, the envelope was empty. My parents thought I had died so my father jumped into his car and he drove as fast as he could to my aunt's. When he saw me..." Lida glanced up at the guard at the door. The woman always had her arms crossed and that twisted look on her face. She shouted the order to be quiet.

Lida bit her lip. She made a few more bullets. The guard tightened her arms around herself and when she finally looked in the other direction, Lida lowered her voice though any of the others could have told the story. They all knew it by heart.

"When Bat'ko saw me, he grabbed me, lifted me way into the sky, and hugged me so tight I thought I'd stop breathing. I don't think he even said hello to my aunt. He put me in the car and I sat in his lap all the way home. When we got to Kyiv, he set me on top of the dining table, turning me round over and over. He gave me one big hug after another. Then..."

"Then...?" Marina, Katia and Jacek all whispered. This was always where the surprise came.

Lida smiled down at the bullet in hand.

"He gave you candy," Jacek started.

"He gave you a tomato," Marina whispered.

Katia looked up at the ceiling and put a finger to her temple. "He gave you a...a...an elephant."

All four of them giggled.

The woman dropped her arms and huffed. Again, the orders to be quiet, to work faster.

All four bent over their bullets.

"No," Lida whispered. "He gave me chocolates."

Marina took in a breath. Katia sighed. Jacek rubbed his belly, and his mouth opened wide into a lopsided "O."

Lida made three more bullets then asked Marina, "What do you remember from Before?"

"I remember when I was a baby," she said. "I remember my mother putting me into a bassinet and we were on a train or a tram. Everyone was singing. I was wearing a little yellow coat with big buttons. When the singing started my mother covered me with a blanket and when she removed the blanket, we were outside where it was warm. I remember flowers."

"My mother says that home is where the sun rises," Katia said.

Lida looked at her.

Jacek said to Marina, "Nobody can remember when they're a baby."

Marina blinked at him. "I can."

"I once had a coat with silver buttons," Katia said.

Lida smiled.

"I wore it all the way here."

Nobody had to ask Katia what happened to the coat. It had happened to all of them. To Lida's green coat a year ago, to Jacek's clothes some weeks later, to Marina's dress last winter and now Katia's pink coat.

Lida turned to Jacek. "If we remember anything, Jacek, it's always the good things. Even if we were only babies."

It was dark when Lida and the others returned to the barracks. None of the adults were back. Lida lay on the thin mattress and waited and much later, she watched her mother's shadow moving against the window before she lay down next to her.

Lida whispered, "Matusia, where is Bat'ko? Have you seen him?" She had waited, had counted the days. Maybe, after thirty-two, it was proper to ask her mother again and her mother could answer.

Her mother did not answer, so Lida asked once more, and this time her mother said, "You barely have a mother left, child. Don't ask about your father again."

Lida watched her mother breathing, sometimes hovering her hand over her face until she felt her exhale. When it grew lighter outside, Lida sat up. A few of the other women were also sitting up. Some looked very confused. Some lay with their eyes open. Others were watching the door. But everyone had to know what Lida knew. It was late and the guards had not come. Where were the guards?

One woman looked at another, then another and slowly everyone was sitting up—the mothers and the children—and Lida shook her mother's shoulder.

"Matusia, wake up. Something is wrong."

The door flew open. A guard stormed in. A second one. They waved their guns at them.

"*Raus! Alle! Schnell!*"

She knew this routine. She knew the words. She understood many languages now. All in all, she knew to keep quiet, to do as ordered, to get out. And be quick about it. Lida grabbed her mother's hand.

Outside, the air was buzzing. There were thunderclaps in the far distance. Matusia's grip was strong. Lida looked up at the sky but it was blue and there were no clouds and the sun was angled so that the frost had already begun melting. There was the heavy crunch of boots on gravel as many soldiers ran to the bunkers. Lida and her mother were pushed into line. Across from her, Lida saw Jacek. He was pressed between his mother and another woman. And Katia. Katia was at the front of their line. Lida tried to look for Marina but the women pushed her forward and Lida had to walk.

"Where are we going?" Lida asked.

She hated it when her mother did not answer her. She stopped and stamped her foot but her mother came behind her and shoved her forward.

The guards were spread out across a long stretch of yard surrounded by woods. A long distance away, Lida saw a lake. The guards were lifting something off the ground. Iron grates. And Lida backed away, yanking her mother's hand with her. A camp guard was lowering Marina into a pit almost on the other end of the yard. The soldiers hurried the others from her group to another pit. Her mother and several others were pushed away, and led to a third hole in the ground.

Lida let go of her mother's hand. Her feet were stuck to the ground. Someone shoved her hard and she fell onto her knees. Matusia called for her, came back, scooped her up and then led her to the mouth in the ground. Lida kicked out as someone took her away from her mother and lifted her up into the air. She screamed as her mother went into the pit and screamed again when the arms of her mother reached for her from below. She was still screaming when she hit the ground and her mother covered her mouth. Lida bit the hand and her mother slapped her.

The grate was back over the hole above their heads. They were buried alive. She, her mother, and a lot of others from the camp. Everyone was looking up. All the faces were looking at the sky above them. Another clap and rumble of thunder. Lida heard a bird call and saw several fly from the trees whose branches stretched above the pit. The birds flew away to where she could no longer see them. She closed her eyes, and strained to hear the birds singing in the woods, in the poplars and aspens. In spring, she liked the bright green haloes that formed around the budding branches. Lida remembered the Dnipro River where she and her mother had taken long strolls, the willow branches she liked to walk under. She could remember that the chestnut blossoms looked like candelabras and that linden trees smelled sweet.

Lida turned to find Jacek, or Marina, or Katia in the group, so that she could say, "See, we *do* only remember the good things," but she did not find any of them there.

Another rumble of thunder, followed by another boom right after that. The birds stopped singing.

It was very quiet. A few people sat down against the earth walls. Others began to talk in quiet whispers. A woman balled up near Matusia's feet and began shaking. Lida was used to all the different languages but she understood little of what anyone was really saying, what they all meant.

Her mother put her hands on Lida's shoulders, then drew Lida to her, and covered her ears.

"They're going to shoot us," Lida heard someone say in Russian. She turned her head to the voice. Her mother tried to cover her ears again but Lida shook them off.

Another woman said, "You're right. They don't want any witnesses."

"The Russians must be coming," the first person said.

"And what good is that?" someone else cried. "The Communists won't treat us any better! They may as well shoot us..."

The woman at Matusia's feet wailed again.

"Shut up," Matusia said angrily. Lida clung to her. "All of you just shut up, now," she said again. She sounded tired this time.

Lida hugged her mother tightly and her mother bent over her, whispering, "Hail Mary, full of grace, the Lord is with thee..." They slid down to the earth and Lida crawled into her mother's lap so that she could rock her.

After the thunder, lightning followed. Short, crackling

bursts, over and over. Lida screamed, buried her head into her mother as far as she could go.

"Make the storm stop," Lida cried.

"That's not a storm," a woman said. As if Lida was a stupid child.

"What is it then?" another woman asked sharply.

"Tanks. Artillery."

The people in the pit began repeating the same word in a number of languages: the Soviets.

The camp guards were returning. They were shouting to each other in German. They neared the pits and Lida saw someone walk past. Shortly after, there were short spurts of gunfire. From another part of the field, the same noise. Screams rose from the ground from far away. Screams rose from the pit Lida was in.

"They're killing us!"

"No, they can't be. The Russians are *here*."

More gunfire and more screams.

"They're coming for us. We're witnesses!"

A high-pitched screech pierced the air. The Germans above started yelling again. Another explosion and dirt rained through the grate. Matusia slammed Lida against the wall of the pit and extended her arms as if to trap Lida there between her and the wall. People behind her mother pushed and shoved. They scrambled over one another, trying to reach the grate above them. The ground vibrated and moaned. Lida screamed. And then the world shattered. Lida was lifted into the air, the sensation not unlike when Bat'ko used to toss her over his head. Except he was not there to catch her.

This is death. She felt nothing. *Sleep.*

A high-pitched ringing. Bees droning. Alarm bells. Sirens. The bells of St. Andrews in Kyiv.

Her mother's voice was far away, as if Lida was in a tin can and her mother was talking to her through it. Fingers. Toes.

Tingling like when she used to kneel too long on the floor, playing with her dolls, and her leg fell asleep.

"Lida, get up, now! We *have to go!* God, help me. Get up, child!"

Lida blinked, she choked and coughed. She spit out dirt. She was standing and her mother was shaking her. Shadows moved all around her. On the ground, Lida saw gray shapes beneath heaps of dirt. Someone looked like a doll she had once pulled apart. Her father had been so angry with her about that. Then she was running, fresh air hurting her lungs. She was running, her arm outstretched, her mother pulling her. Lida tried to keep up, tried to get her legs to follow. She stumbled. She fell. Her mother's face next to her, telling her to get up, to run, in God's name, get up. Lida tried. They fell against a truck that was turned over like a beetle on its back, the wheels going round and round. A helmet lay on the ground next to Lida. She closed her eyes, and when she felt the pull, felt the tug of her mother's hand, she made her legs unstick from the ground. The next time she looked—really looked-looked—they were deep in a forest.

"Where are we going?"

"Straight ahead," was all her mother said.

But Before was behind them. "How will we find Bat'ko," Lida asked, "if we are going where the sun sets?"

Another day. Another bridge. Another town. Where there are factories, Lida's mother said, there is work. They had followed the muddy River Spree for hours and hours before Matusia knocked on a door where Lida could read the sign in German. Room for rent. Their search was over.

Frau Fessler had a single room with one bed, a dresser, and a shared toilet for them. Lida slept, they said, for days. Some time later, Frau Fessler also found two Ukrainian women in the village, who worked in the laundry. The women came by to meet Matusia and Lida. For the first time in a long-long-long time, Lida's mother smiled and laughed. When the two Ukrainian women came, Lida stopped smiling when they told Matusia that they were hoping the Americans would come before the Red Army. Bat'ko was a Red Army commander, and Matusia had said that, if he had escaped like they had, he would come for them with the whole army. The Ukrainian women then asked Matusia about the camp. Matusia told them about things Lida could not remember, did not know, and did not like. She went up to her room and crawled under the covers until the women left and Matusia came upstairs.

"Frau Fessler said you could go to school here. She said that she could help register you, that there are lots of other children from all over in the school." In the afternoons, she said, Lida could help Frau Fessler by working around the house.

"She agreed we could pay less rent that way," Matusia finished as if the matter were settled. She was brushing her hair at the dresser.

"I don't want to go to school."

Matusia dropped her hand into her lap. It made a slapping sound. "You would be with other children your age. Like Before."

It was nothing like Before, Lida said. She didn't want anything that was anything like the camp either.

"I have to work," Matusia said, and she started brushing her hair again.

"I want to be here with you."

"I have to work,"—she turned around—"so that we can eat, so that we can have coupons, and get food. Frau Fessler does not have enough for us and she does not want you home alone all day."

Lida's teeth chattered. She shivered. "I don't want to."

Matusia stood up. She put Lida into the chair in front of the mirror and began brushing. "You don't have to go now. You'll go in a week. Or two. But you will go."

Lida's voice was higher. "But—"

"No buts," Matusia snapped. "When the war comes to an end, we need to stay put if your father is to find us."

Lida's eyes widened. She stared at her mother. She had a hundred million thousand questions but her mother was pulling at the tangles and knots in Lida's long, dark hair and she said, "Now, we're going to make sure you look pretty again." She put her hands on Lida's shoulders and bent to her, their faces next to one another in the mirror. "Like Before. Then when your father finds us, we can tell him what a good girl you've been."

The first two days in school were horrible and Lida decided that she was still in After—that Matusia and she had never really left the other place. The people were not nice to her. The next days, things grew worse. To get to school, she had to pass a checkpoint, where young boys in uniforms carried rifles and glared at Lida beneath their caps. The students teased Lida, poking her in the back, spitting in her hair, pulling it, and calling her names.

In the mornings, Matusia woke her to get ready and was gone in the next instant. Here, just like in the camp, Matusia worked from morning until night. Frau Fessler did, too. Lida was alone again. No father. No mother. No adults at all. She missed the children from the camp—Marina, Katia, Jacek—and wondered what had happened to them but when she thought of that day in the pit, remembered the thunder, Lida could not breathe. The sweater she wore—too small for her anyway—choked her around the collar. It squeezed at her chest. She yanked and pulled, but it was tight. She yelled for help. She ripped the sweater off over her head, and flung it on the ground. She fell to the bedroom floor, curled up and cried. She was dying. Certainly that was it. And her mother would find her like this and be sorry that she'd left her here alone.

Later, when she did not die, Lida went down to the kitchen. Her bun for breakfast and her bun for dinner were on the countertop. She was not allowed to eat the second one until five o'clock. Lida looked at both buns. A schedule, her mother said, was necessary to overcome the starvation. Lida did not care. She grabbed the first bun, lifted the butter crock and ripped a piece of the bun off to run it over the sides and scoop out what butter there was left. Then she shoved the whole piece into her mouth. She started on the second one, just a bite. Then a next piece. And again. And then it was all gone and it was still morning and she had left the crock dry and clean. Fresh tears came again, making the bread in her mouth salty and sweet all at once.

Her stomach rumbled. She looked around the kitchen. Maybe there was something else to eat. A pretty tin was on the shelf next to the plates and cups and saucers. It was decorated with different colored flowers on a golden background. She swallowed the last mouthful of bread and pushed a stool to the shelf, and climbed it to retrieve the tin. She turned the tin round and round, touching the different flowers. Something moved inside. She pulled the lid off, and a rich smell floated out. It wasn't strong like Lida remembered it but it was familiar. In fact, she had to dip her nose into the can and suck the smell out, but there it was: coffee.

The bag wasn't very big. There were probably only a hundred coffee beans but she remembered how the Ukrainian women had talked about trading, how "ridiculous" coffee was worth these days. She thought of how her mother had started to collect cigarettes from people at the laundry where she worked, pretending that she smoked. Instead, at night, Matusia carefully wrapped the cigarettes into her pocket and she would return at night with a bit of cheese or a wilted vegetable. Lida's mouth watered.

When she stepped out into the street, Lida patted the little sack containing the coffee beans. She wandered toward the town center and then passed the shops. First the baker, who still had two loaves of bread left. She'd just had bread. Then there was the butcher with his one loop of sausage in the window. A man walked out with a newspaper-wrapped bundle and Lida watched him as he turned the corner, a delicious smell lingering behind him. The sausage link. That was it.

Lida stepped inside and went to the counter. There was nobody in the shop, but she could hear something like a machine in the back room. She wandered over to stand at the window, beneath the loop of sausage.

A big man stepped up behind her. He was wearing a blood-smeared apron. "What are you doing?"

Lida held the sack of beans out.

He took a step forward. "What is that?"

Lida held it up and pointed to the sausage.

The butcher laughed. "No, no! Coupons! Do you have coupons?"

She shook her head. Only her mother understood the coupons.

"Sorry, little miss. I can't help you."

Lida left the shop, putting her beans back into the pocket of her dress. The shops were not going to help her. Perhaps she could find someone who wanted coffee in the neighborhood. Someone who had something like—Lida smiled—chocolate.

A woman, still dressed in her housecoat, stepped out of her back door in one of the alleyways which Lida had turned into. The lady dropped a bag into a nearby garbage pail and then shuffled back inside. Lida stopped and eyed the bag, then spotted a girl sitting on the stoop. The girl's attention was focused on something in her lap.

For a moment, the little girl stared at her. Lida decided the girl had the most beautiful hair she had ever seen. It was long and straight, and it glowed golden. This girl's mother must have brushed her hair a thousand times every night. Lida opened the wooden gate and went into the garden.

"*Tag,*" the little girl whispered. She was dressing a rag doll in bandages.

"*Was ist das?*" Lida asked, trying to sound like the butcher. Everyone laughed at her pronunciation in school.

The girl looked up. "*Eine Puppe.*"

"*Puppe?*"

"*Ja, Puppe.*"

Lida held her hand out and the girl placed the bandaged rag doll into it.

"*Sie hat Schmerzen.*"

How did the doll get hurt, Lida wanted to know. She did not know the words. Instead, she could only ask what the doll's name was.

"Ilse," said the girl.

Ilse was a pretty name, Lida said, and the girl smiled. Her name was Katrin and she was going to be Lida's friend.

When Matusia returned home late at night, Lida heard Frau Fessler call her into the kitchen.

It was a warm, spring evening, and Lida was sitting outside the house in the back courtyard. Ilse was in agreement with everything that Lida thought. She held a small piece of bread to Ilse's mouth and Lida prompted her to eat. "*Nicht so schnell, mein Kind. Du bist verhungert,*" she said. Frau Fessler had said that to her many times before. Not so fast, my child, you are starving.

When the back door opened, Matusia's shadow fell over

Lida. For a moment, it was as if they were back in the work camp because Matusia wore that same look when she was tired and going to be easily angry. "Where did you get that doll?"

Lida hid the doll behind her back.

"I asked you, where you got the doll from."

"I found it."

"Where?"

"There was a trash can." She was not lying.

"Lida, do you recognize this?" Her mother was holding the pretty tin can, tipped so that she could see it was empty.

Lida shook her head.

"Did you take the coffee?"

Lida's eyes stung. She blinked.

"Do you know how hard I had to work for that coffee?" Matusia's voice was like an owl's screech. "Do you know how many hours of washing bloodied uniforms that takes? Just for a coupon for coffee? We have nothing else, child! Nothing! If it weren't for Frau Fessler, we would only be eating coffee soup! Now, tell me again, where did you get that doll?"

Lida felt something boiling up in her. She did not care about coffee. She did not care if her mother ever came home again. She had Ilse now. She did not need her mother.

Lida started for the back gate. Her mother was too quick for her. She grabbed the bandaged doll, gave it a disgusted look, then held it up again. "Are you going to eat your doll? Or better yet, is *she* going to feed you?"

"I hate you!"

Her mother's mouth opened. Her eyes narrowed. Her teeth clenched. Matusia shoved the doll back at Lida. "You will go, immediately, to where you got this doll and bring back our coffee."

The "No" on Lida's tongue was there but it failed to come out. She slunk to the gate and made her way to Katrin's house.

When Katrin's mother appeared in the doorway, Lida's face was crusted with tears.

Katrin appeared at her mother's skirts and Lida handed her the doll, wailing in Ukrainian, then in Russian, then in German.

"Kaffee?" Katrin's mother said. *"Haben wir ihren Kaffee, Schatz?"*

Katrin nodded and dashed into the house, returning with the bag of coffee. She handed it to Lida, and Lida sniffed, trying not to cry again. Katrin's mother clucked a little and put a hand on Lida's head, murmuring words that made Lida feel better even if she did not understand them all.

The next morning, Matusia surprised her by telling her she would be going into work later and would walk Lida to school.

"I can go by myself," Lida said.

Her mother paused from brushing her hair and faced Lida. "I know you can. I just thought you might like some company."

Lida shrugged. She wanted to play with Katrin, not go to school. "I really can go by myself."

Her plan was to return to Katrin's house and play with her until she had to do her chores in the afternoon. She imagined what it would be like to live with Katrin and her mother. Maybe they had food, more food than here. Maybe they had meat, and things that Lida missed so very much. Maybe they would even let her live with them.

But when Lida came into town, something was very different. Lida saw that the bridge was blocked off. There were big bags stacked on top of each other and there were real soldiers here now—not just the boys—and the bridge was barricaded with barbed wire. She looked at the buildings before her. The shutters and doors were all closed even though it was a nice, spring day. Lida heard the school bell ringing but she did not see any children. The bell continued to ring. Then a siren.

Lida looked up above where the buzzing was coming from. Airplanes. Her feet were stuck to the ground.

The soldiers threw themselves behind the barricades. Guns pointed at the sky. Townspeople scattered every which way through the street. Someone tried to talk to her, tried to pull her. Matusia? The thunder was coming again. She could not hear what her mother was saying over the thunder in the air.

Lida felt a familiar sensation, of being lifted off the ground and carried. Her father putting her into the black car. Bat'ko lifting her onto the dining room table and turning her around over and over. Bat'ko, lifting her into the air and over his head. She was in Before when other men did this to her. They had put her in the back of a truck and her mother and father had both covered her as St. Andrew's bells rang and the green dome grew smaller. She had been lifted again when Bat'ko put her into her mother's arms in the world of After and disappeared the next moment. Lida had been lifted and carried and dragged, time and again, by people who tried to take her to places she did not want to—could not—go. And still they put her there. The bunker. The yard. The forest. Over the bridge and into this town. And now someone was carrying her again but this time to the river. This time, they were taking her to those bags at the base of the bridge. And her mother was running in front of her.

Lida moaned when the ground lost all give. She and whoever carried her tumbled down the grassy bank. She collided with the earth. Her body deflated, all the air gone. Machine guns rattled bullets into the air. The airplanes showered bullets back. All those trays and trays of bullets. She fought for breath. A heavy weight crushed her. The noises died down. Then air. Air, finally, air. She sucked it in, then drank the air.

"Are you hurt? Are you all right?" two voices were asking her.

Her mother was next to her, lips moving next to Lida's face, asking the questions, touching her. Lida felt the weight on top of her shifting, felt the hand covering her head when she tried to raise it. She lay very-very still. Speak again, she willed the other voice. Speak one more time.

"Stay put. Don't move," Bat'ko said. "I've got you now."

He slowly rolled her over and she threw her arms around her father's neck.

Lida decided she would call this part After-After.

AN INVENTORY OF MERCIES
BAVARIA, 1945

i. The Canvases

The first signs of spring are buried beneath the rubble and dust. If Stepan had to give the color a name, it would be "fool's gray." He would squeeze a little of each of his oils onto the palette and mix them into this one color. Not quite black, not quite brown—just a mass compound of all that had once been pure and beautiful and innocent. As the train churns west to Nuremberg, each town's station is crammed with people desperate to flee. And when the train does not slow down, Stepan is afraid they will throw themselves at it or before it. He sees their faces as the carriage passes by—angry, desperate faces.

Town after German town has been transformed into a jagged, gaping display of blasted mortar, cables, and steel, smoke exhaling from the bellies of interiors. There are always hints of what a building once housed: a bed frame dangling from the third floor of a bombed-out apartment building; the *Möbel-* missing its *-haus* on a furniture store sign; a factory that might once have produced harmless kitchen appliances but yesterday was suspected of producing artillery and reduced to the consequences. He has witnessed similar scenes since the Blitzkrieg—since the first tanks blew a hole through his studio in L'viv, followed by the bombing of the gallery that had exhibited his paintings. There was nearly nothing to salvage afterwards. He took the attack personally back then. He scoffs at the idea now.

The cityscapes are interrupted by an almost utopian countryside. It is a cruel taunt, a callous reminder of the trips he and Olena took to the Carpathians to visit Tosia. They'd often stopped so that he could sketch out the Galician scenery. Olena had placed a journal in her lap and captured the landscape in stories and music, while he composed in oils. *Women working in fields. Mountain shepherds. Galician church.* He is good at the details: the embroidered blouses in green, gold, and red on the women, the timber church with the onion dome, the shepherds in woolen capes and leather moccasins. He has not painted in half a year—since the restoration of the chapel in Czechoslovakia—but he has carried what he has all this way. Twelve canvases are all that remain.

Once in a while, Stepan catches sight of people on the country lanes—in groups usually—heading in every which way, trying to escape the Allies' pincers. The drifters the trains cannot take. All of them—on this train and the civilians out there—are the immaterial cost of war. He asks himself whether he will be a number tallied in the list of survivors or of the casualties when the governments sit down to calculate.

The wastes of war are heaped alongside a road, and the litter of someone's life is strewn just along the rail tracks. Someone's suitcase either fell or has been thrown out the window. There is no room in the carriages, and they are crammed in beyond imaginable. The other passengers in the car are made up of veterans and shady men, frail grandmothers and grandfathers, exhausted mothers and their shell-shocked children. They all fought to get onto this transport. The station in Berlin had been a scene of mass hysteria, a mob gone berserk. People had turned to violence—men yanking women off the trains to take a spot, women thrashing their children into submission. Animals, all of them. He might have done the same. How else are they all here? Yes, he might have done the same.

He looks at his young son, Roman, born the day before the Blitzkrieg. He dozes in the arms of his aunt Tosia, one thumb stuck in his mouth. Yurko is sleeping fitfully next to Olena, trying to get comfortable. Stepan watches the boy's chest rise and fall, and Stepan's heart clenches. The fact that the artists in Berlin managed his family's escape from the camp in Wilhelmshagen was nothing short of a miracle. Yurko would have died, and Stepan would have certainly lost Olena to grief or madness.

Tosia moves, and Stepan watches as she reaches over the aisle and lays a hand on his bouncing knee.

"Is it that obvious?" he asks.

"Every time you look at them."

She withdraws the touch and gently places Roman's slipped foot back into her lap before closing her eyes. Sleep is all they yearn for—every single one of these people on this transport just wants to sleep. And how many now yearn for Hitler's demise?

He shakes his head. His attempt to reach Switzerland, to sit out the war with the diaspora of artists, is far—very far—from where they are now. Every time he takes inventory of his current situation, Stepan comes to the same conclusion: everything that this family has lost up to now is inconsequential compared to the simple fact that they are still together. It is another miracle that they are on this train. He lightly touches his breast pocket to assure himself that the packet of travel and work permits, which Myron secured for them, are still real. The identification papers have transformed them into Polish citizens. Poland will likely remain free after the war, his friends in

Berlin predicted, but Ukraine? Doubtful. *You don't want to be repatriated, Stepan.*

Myron is painting propaganda posters near Munich. Though the work permit does not specify whether Stepan is expected to do the same, if he has learned anything on this journey, it is this: he will give up everything—including his principles, including his painting, his life—to keep his family alive.

Just as in Berlin, it appears the American and British forces are taking shifts to bomb Nuremberg. It is that unrecognizable. He'd stopped here on his way to the art college in Paris over two decades ago. This is not that city now. As the train approaches the station, Stepan sees the noble, old buildings have been destroyed. Families live in decrepit shelters made of rubble. As soon as Stepan helps his family off the train, he takes up the cases and looks for the connection to Munich. A siren's blare pulls him up short. It is followed by panicked shouts and screams. At any moment the whistle and high pitches of falling bombs will follow. He has no idea where to go. He whirls around to make sure the women and children are with him. And then he sees it. Across the tracks, the sign—BUNKER—with yellow arrows pointing at camouflaged doorways. His heart drops at the sight of the pressing crowd. A fistfight between two men breaks out. A German officer puts a stop to it, forces the crowd to move out of the way so that soldiers can take their place in line first.

Olena clutches Stepan's hand. She has seen it too. And the song in the sky has started. It is Berlin all over again, and they are in a train station. At the end of the station, Stepan sees a depot yard filled with freight cars.

Tosia wastes no time. She drops between two cars on the tracks and yanks Roman from the edge of the platform. Stepan follows her, turning to pick up Yurko, who will not let go of his mother's hand.

"Olena, come," Stepan begs.

But his wife is looking worriedly at the crowd. The people are pushing and shoving their way to a single elevator that will take them beneath the ground. She shakes her head, still on the platform. There is a hissing sound, a pop, and Stepan realizes the train is going to move. Between the two carriages, Tosia—with Roman in her arms—shouts for them to hurry. Stepan yanks Yurko into his arms, and Olena jumps down onto the rails. They scramble over to the other side just as the train pulls away, brimming with people. Still more passengers cling to its sides, to anything they can hold on to. The ground shakes beneath him, followed by another explosion. It is still far away. The train blasts its whistle, a different sound from the warning shrieks above, and flees the domed station.

Stepan takes Yurko into his arms and presses into the crowd. On tiptoe, he sees that there is no hope. If the planes fly over the train station and drop their bombs on the depot outside, they will all be buried here. He presses Yurko to him, covering his head. His son whimpers, wraps his arms around Stepan's neck and he cannot breathe. Stepan feels someone poking him on the shoulder. He shrugs it off, intent on moving forward. He is not about to be distracted by anyone. Someone yanks on his arm, and Stepan shrugs it off and glances irritably over his shoulder—and freezes.

The man is wearing a black coat, a black cap with the *Totenkopf* and the eagle. Stepan knows these uniforms well.

They'd fled Wilhelmshagen. They are fugitives and somehow—somehow!—this officer knows that.

"Kommen Sie mit."

A laugh bubbles up in Stepan. He shakes his head. "I'm staying with my family." He says the word for family in German.

The senior officer—about Stepan's age—waves the rest of the family over. *"Alle. Bringen Sie die gesamte Familie mit."*

Stepan says in Polish, "We are Polish. We are Polish citizens." This man cannot possibly want to check their papers now! The door is just right there. They need to get below ground.

The officer is not having it. He wants Stepan to follow him. Stepan wants to shout, to fight. Tosia has stepped out of line, Olena next to her, a child in each of their arms. They stare at this officer with the same look of disbelief, of terror, of doom. The officer yanks on Stepan's coat and gestures again that he wants him to follow. He points to something. Stepan looks. It is another door, and there is an elevator. Army personnel and officers are gathered there.

Stepan does not think. He moves. There is a screeching at the end of the station, and he can see planes heading for them, like geese about to make a landing.

The bunker is four levels down, and the dust and rubble is falling around their heads, one explosion after another. If it is falling here, then how are the other three levels above? How will the civilians above them survive this onslaught? Certainly all their days are finished.

The lamps buzz, dim, go out, and come back on. Over and over. Sometimes there is nothing. And no one stirs. The air is thick with the stench of sweat and urine. The children whimper before anything happens. Everyone jumps with the next impact. Olena spasms, as if in sleep. Stepan checks and is astonished. She is indeed asleep. Yurko has also grown heavy in his arms.

Save for the occasional pauses, the thundering never stops. And nobody attempts to leave during the breaks in between.

The Nazi officer's eyes dart to Stepan in the flickering light, then rest on him when the glow is steady again. *"Wie heißen Sie?"*

"Stepan Lucyk," Stepan says.

The officer sticks out his hand. "Oswald Luger."

Stepan hesitates. A German officer never introduces himself like this. Still, he reaches over Yurko and takes it. In broken German, he asks Luger why him? Why had he found him and brought Stepan's family here?

Luger blinks, looks away for a moment. To Stepan he says, *"Sie haben Hilfe gebraucht."* You needed help.

Stepan does not know what to say to that. He remembers the day he and his family were diverted from their path to Switzerland. The transport trucks that crunched to a stop in the dawn. The Czech and Slovak villagers stepping out of their cottages, despair written on their faces. They'd been herded onto cattle trucks, all of them, and taken to Gdansk. The Soviets had broken through the lines, and the family—slaves, then—were hustled towards Berlin.

The lights go out for the last time, and it is dark. He feels Olena wake up next to him, and now she is shaking. Tosia soothes her. And then the swearing begins. The Nazis in this bunker—and there are many—raise their voices, shout into the darkness, and Stepan begins to understand that they are not cursing the Allies. They are cursing Hitler. Stepan feels something growing, spreading and shaking itself out within him, like bird wings. It is hope.

The group must climb through stairways and tunnels. They are blocked by rubble and must turn around. The Nazis lead them to many other exits. Finally, like moles, Stepan and the others clamber out from the belly of Nuremberg some distance from the train station. The first thing is the stench. Olena chokes and covers her mouth. Tosia pinches her nose. Everyone is turning, trying to orientate themselves in this new world. Stepan's assumption was right. Those who had managed to get to the civilian bunkers had had no chance of survival. The station—with its rounded dome—is no more. In its place is a crater. Up the tracks, a derailed train lies turned over, bodies strewn about. It's the train that had tried to flee.

Fires burn everywhere. Tosia makes the sign of the cross. Olena weeps openly. Stepan must as well as he pictures his family in that crater or on that train. He finds Luger and bows, bends over, pumps his hand. Luger has saved their lives, and Stepan owes him for it. Luger closes his eyes and shakes his head. He directs Stepan to the most likely place they might find a bus that will take them to Munich. Stepan cannot thank him enough. Luger, his cap tucked beneath his arm, takes out a handkerchief from his pocket and turns away.

Stepan leads his family through the rubble. And out of the city. They just walk. And walk. It is night. The boys are complaining of hunger. Olena is silent as she walks next to him. Tosia distracts the boys by explaining what has just happened, where they are going, and how very lucky they are. She leads them into a prayer of thanks. Sometime later, Stepan stops short. He grabs Olena's hand. In the dark, she catches her breath, turns her head back toward Nuremberg.

"Stepan?" Olena asks. "What is it?"

Stepan cannot speak it. He faces what is ahead. A tree-lined road, the fields, the stars above. A sign indicates they are entering a new town. Perhaps they will be lucky and find mercy again—a place to sleep, food, a reprieve. Stepan does not let go of her hand. He takes it to his lips. He kisses it. He has forgotten the case with his canvases.

ii. Potatoes and Paintbrushes

"Butterbrot?" The round woman smiles at Yurko and hands him the roll with butter on it.

The bus jostles them all together. It is the strangest contraption any of the family has seen. It runs on steam produced by a wood burner. The driver stopped some kilometers ago and picked them up. He wears *Lederhosen*, and Yurko has already called him St. Nicholas for the bushy white beard and the cheery manner. Indeed it is like Christmas.

Yurko looks at Stepan, then takes the bread. The woman gives one to Roman as well. They are her last rolls.

Stepan smiles at her, says, *"Danke sehr."* Yurko holds up a piece to him. Stepan shakes his head. Olena tells the boy to eat it. Stepan sees she is also hungry. They are all hungry. They are tired, dirty, and move as if in a dream. But they are also all smiling.

"Ein Sack Holz," the driver cries to Stepan. The bus sputters as he shifts gears.

Stepan rises, fetches one of the bags of wood chips, and opens the burner. He shovels the chips in. When he offered to pay the driver some *Marks* to take them to Munich, the driver said, *"Ich fahre. Du arbeitest. Ich sage, ein Sack Holz, Du, Holz rein. Verstanden?"*

Stepan understands him. As the only man on the bus, Stepan is happy the driver employs him to keep the bus moving.

He takes his seat again, and the women laugh. Roman repeats with a childlike bellow, "Hoz! Hoz!" He indicates to Stepan he should stand up again and put more wood chips in. Stepan runs a hand over his son's head and kisses him. The German women on the bus smile.

Yurko asks a boy if he can look at his toy soldier. The mother pokes her son, and the boy cautiously hands it to Yurko. Yurko is careful with it.

The woman across from Stepan asks how old the children are. He holds up both his palms and adds one more digit for Yurko. He turned eleven last month. Roman will be four in June. She points to Roman's hair and wiggles her eyebrows, rolls her eyes, and laughs. Red hair, big spirit. Olena smiles. Roman has her chestnut-red hair, but both of them are gentle and mild mannered. Yurko looks like him, Stepan tells the woman. He tells her that Yurko also has his eyes—for artistic composition.

They ride like this for some time, when one of the women recites a nursery rhyme. Roman sits up. He claps his hands in rhythm. The bus sputters to a stop, and Stepan stands up to grab another bag of wood chips, but the driver turns to them and indicates with a nod of his head that they should all get off. Stepan is once again struck at how obedient everyone is—him included—asking so few questions and simply following the crowd. This is how it worked. This is why they are here.

The bus driver stands with legs spread out, woolen socks pulled up to his kneecaps, those *Lederhosen*, and the big belly over the waist. In the far-off distance, an inferno on the horizon. Munich.

Olena clutches Stepan's elbow. Tosia shakes her head. The driver and the women are all grim-faced now. He gestures to Stepan to come over to him. They talk with their hands and in two languages. Where does Stepan want to go? Prien. To Chiemsee. Stepan withdraws the work permit, gives him Myron's address. The driver clicks his tongue and grumbles something like an apology. He scratches his head. He talks to the other women. They list off other names. Mostly Munich. But nobody here is going to Munich any longer.

Finally the driver makes a decision, slaps Stepan on the back, and smiles. *"Ein Sack Holz, mein Herr!"* Stepan hurries to the stove, hears the women and the children taking their seats again, and shovels wood chips into the oven.

When the bus stops in Prien, Stepan hugs the bus driver, as

do both the boys. The women are surprised, Olena backing
away as the Bavarian strides over to her with wide-open arms.
He offers his hand instead but then turns to Tosia and wraps
her in a bear hug and spins her around. She laughs loud and
clear. Olena joins her, slapping her thigh. Stepan has not heard
that laugh in a long time. It takes him back to the hunter's lodge
in the mountains, the nights by the fire, the singing, the dancing.
The day he fell in love with Olena. He thanks the driver again,
is very sad to see him go, but they have reached their next
destination.

Another round of embraces follows when Myron finally reaches
them. Stepan almost believes they might have made it. They
might have survived. And when Myron tells them that American forces are just south of them, the entire group lets out a
cheer.

This part of Bavaria is spectacular. To the south, the Alps
form the border to Austria. Whole villages with red steeples or
onion domes are scattered about on the horizon. Medieval
castles and fortresses are set into the mountainsides, or near the
lakes, or on the edge of forests. Chiemsee is so large it has an
island that is home to a convent. There are boats on the lake,
and fishermen. It is as if this area has never encountered a
battle. Stepan can hardly believe it, but Myron assures him they
have seen trouble here too. Berchtesgaden is not far away.

Myron has secured a home for them. It is not allowed, he
explains. They must register all refugees, but he is finished with
the bureaucracy of this country. A farmer has agreed to take
three of them in, no questions asked. His name is Herr Koch,
and Frau Wechsel, the neighbor, can take two. The family and
the boys discuss who will stay where, and Roman will stay with

Stepan and Olena. Yurko and Tosia will stay at Frau Wechsel's down the road.

They drive through luscious countryside, the spring air laden with lilacs and magnolia. They enter a town, and Stepan reads the sign: *HÖHENSTADT*. They pull into a farmyard. Everything here is picture perfect, untouched by that cruel and foolish war around them. Herr Koch steps out of the house. He is small, dressed in a blue smock and a cap, and has the face of someone who has weathered many bad days. But his eyes are alight and are kind, and Herr Koch explains through Myron that the family will be working on the farm, picking potatoes.

"Potatoes!" Olena cries. She pulls Yurko to her absentmindedly and says to Stepan, "We will never starve again as long as we have potatoes."

Frau Wechsel comes by to help in the house and to cook. Herr Koch is a widower and now childless as well. His sons fell on the Eastern Front. Stepan and he look at one another, and Stepan feels he understands something more about the past few days, about all the mercies they have been granted.

It takes them only a little bit of time to ease the stress, the burdens and the sadness from their shoulders. It takes them more time to relax and to get into a routine that does not require scrounging for food or fearing what is around the corner.

After two weeks pass, Olena and Tosia are in the kitchen, joking with one another, scolding the boys for this and that, but always with smiles and gentleness. They enjoy Frau Wechsel's company, learn how to make *Knödel*, and Olena teaches her how to make *varenyky*. There are ham, potatoes, and early lettuces.

One day Herr Koch arrives to the farm with a large sack and walks past them all sitting in the kitchen and into the bathroom. Stepan rises to offer help, but Herr Koch has already sliced the heavy sack and is now dumping its contents into the bathtub.

There is a sound like soft gravel against the ceramic. The farmer steps back and lets everyone see what he has done.

Beans. A tub full of beans.

Tosia and Olena look at each other, and Tosia—like a little girl—claps her hands. They will never, ever starve again, she says. It is all that really counts.

Herr Koch grunts, scratches his head, and then with a grin that looks like he's about to tell a secret, he looks at Stepan. *"Und,"* he says, *"der Führer ist tot."* Koch smiles broadly and does a little dance. Frau Wechsel slaps her palms over her face.

"Hitler?" Stepan asks, not believing what he thinks he has understood. He draws a finger over his throat.

Herr Koch puts an index finger to his temple and pulls an imaginary trigger.

Now Olena and Tosia understand. Frau Wechsel repeats it. Hitler is dead.

The next day, the Americans arrive.

He is painting again. At first he tries to reconstruct some of his old paintings. He tries to recapture home, but the act makes his heart break, and his memories are muddled by the darkness he must get through—to propel him back east, to his beloved Ukraine. Olena is also showing signs of melancholy. Tosia has taken to praying more frequently, and she gives daily lessons about the Bible to the children. It is her lifeboat.

Myron finally comes by. He picks Stepan up at Herr Koch's, and they spend the day in the mountains of Berchtesgaden. These trips become more frequent, and over the weeks, the party grows. There are suddenly many Ukrainians among them, some old friends, reunited in this safe zone. And Stepan enjoys it, but it adds to the homesickness and to the uncertainties he harbors about their future. The artists hike with their easels and paints, their sketchpads and oils. He takes the boat to Königssee, paints the jagged crags of Watzemann, the sailboats on the Chiemsee. Sometimes, Olena and Tosia join him, leaving the children with Frau Wechsel, and they have picnics with their companions. Olena has been writing. She has composed a song, too. A love song to the Carpathians, to their home. There is not a dry eye in Myron's cramped sitting room. They are all concerned about their country.

There is other talk. Talk about how the Americans are rounding up refugees, putting them into camps. Stepan swears he will never go to a camp again. He and Koch have already made arrangements. Koch still believes they are Polish. Everyone fears the Red Army. The Soviets are not far away, and Stalin has ordered the Allies to return any of their citizens back to the custody of the Motherland. But Stepan's Motherland stands with a knife at her back, for there is more talk about Stalin's new order. Anyone found on enemy soil will be considered a traitor when returned. It is not safe to go home. Everyone is on a black list now, regardless which side they fought on, which party or faction they supported. Now, they are all simply displaced Ukrainians who are struggling to settle into fake identities. More and more of them are becoming Polish.

"In other words," Stepan murmurs to Olena on his return to Koch's farm, "we are still in danger."

He thinks of Switzerland and decides to write a letter again.

Myron fetches him, and they set up their easels along the fishing dock one fine July day. White puffy clouds dot the sky. The Alps are summer green on the horizon. But Stepan feels like painting people today. There is a feeling of summer holidays. Children run along the beach, playing in the water. A woman in a large-brimmed hat glides her hands over the lake's surface before she dips the rest of herself in. Yes, he wants to paint these people today.

He begins with the small sketchbook, watches, adds the

little yellow dog poking into the reeds after the ducks. He is happy doing this. He is enjoying it, these new studies, these fresh models. A shadow falls over him, and he looks up.

"That's very good," a man in a green uniform says. His German has a foreign accent. "May I?"

Stepan is looking into the face of an officer of the American commanding forces. He silently hands him the sketchbook. The American smiles, shades his eyes, and sighs.

"Are you from here?" he asks in German.

Stepan stands, his heart in his throat. He reaches for his documents in his breast pocket. "Polish," he says, also in German. "Polish citizen." He hands the officer the papers, but the man seems uninterested. He gives a polite smile and looks back at the sketchbook.

"Would you do a portrait?" The officer gestures to the sketchbook, then to himself, then to the sketchbook again. He smiles hopefully. He sticks his hand in his pocket and withdraws some bills. Stepan stares at the American dollars.

Three days later he has more commissions and a brand-new set of beautiful horsehair brushes.

iii. The Restorers

A terrible metallic crunch is followed by a wet hiss. Stepan shoots up in bed. Olena calls for God. A beam of light shines crazily into the window. Stepan's blood runs cold. He goes to the window, but now two beams of light blind him. Upstairs, a door slams. Herr Koch. Then there is pounding from the front entrance. Stepan steps into the hallway, sees the silhouette of a man through the window in the door. The stranger raises his arms and pounds once more. Koch is at the top of the stairs. He has a rifle.

The door blows open, and the figure sways unsteadily for a

moment, props himself against the doorframe, then pushes himself in. Stepan sees he is holding a weapon—a large one.

Koch turns on the light.

It is an American soldier. He has a submachine gun, which he waves about, as if to punctuate his demand. "Schnapps! Schnapps!"

Koch raises the rifle over his head. *"Ich habe keinen Schnaps!"*

The soldier looks wildly at Stepan. His cheeks and nose are splotched red, his eyes roll crazily about. His helmet is tipped back off his head, revealing a high forehead and dark hair.

They don't have any schnapps, Stepan repeats.

The soldier blinks. He says something, and Stepan recognizes the cuss words he's heard on the American base. Olena steps behind Stepan, and the soldier sways, blinks at her. It is the most sober he has looked. He asks her, "Schnapps?"

"Ja," Olena says.

Stepan chokes. Olena waves the soldier into the kitchen behind the stairwell. Koch comes down the stairs. Stepan and he hurry into the kitchen. Olena has pulled out a stool for the soldier and watches as he lowers himself onto it. He lays the submachine gun onto the table. The men stand at the doorway, but Stepan itches to grab the weapon off the table.

A noise behind Stepan causes him to whirl around. Tosia and Frau Wechsel are standing there, clutching the children's hands, and Stepan remembers that Roman had spent the night at Frau Wechsel's. He'd wanted to be with his brother that night. But now they are all here, in this house, with this madman.

Olena has retrieved something out of the back of a cabinet. The cork pops off the bottle. There is a red liquid inside. Koch shakes his head, confounded, and Olena looks at the group. She shrugs.

"Frau Wechsel brought kirsch the other day," she says to Stepan. "We all had a nip. This is what is left."

Hooray for Frau Wechsel, Stepan thinks.

Olena pours the soldier a glass, but he motions for the bottle, sniffs it, makes a face, and tips it to his mouth, draining it. He burps. He puts the bottle down. His head falls onto the table.

Two military policemen later pick up the soldier, assess the damages to the vehicle and Koch's walnut tree, and ask for identification papers.

The next morning, the family is around the breakfast table, discussing the night's events. There is nervous laughter. Olena is a hero. As is Frau Wechsel. She has brought a second bottle of kirsch to calm their nerves. The anxiety is palpable. When will the Americans come back?

They come back. A handful of them. They remove the accordion of a vehicle, they compensate for the walnut tree in local currency, and have chocolates and toys for the children. Yurko says in German that the Americans are fantastic. He asks Stepan to agree with him. Stepan nods.

Before they all leave, one man approaches them. He speaks to Herr Koch. He says he is from the United Nations. They have set up a displaced persons camp in Rosenheim. He points at Stepan and the family. "They are refugees, and all refugees are to be placed in a DP camp."

"But they are Polish," Koch says.

Frau Wechsel says, "They work for us."

The man nods sympathetically. "Polish too. I'm sure we will sort this out. If everything is legitimate, you file for official work status."

Stepan hurries into the house and returns with the work permits. The man nods and sighs. They are no longer valid. Stepan must apply for new work permits with the new government.

As the military convoy leaves, Myron drives into the farmyard. He gets out of the truck, his expression strained and cautious. The Lucyks have been told to pack up their things. They will be retrieved by the UN relief organization in an hour. Myron goes into the house with them. Olena and Tosia are pleading with Frau Wechsel. They do not want to leave. They do not want to go to a camp. Frau Wechsel assures them they will be all right. Myron, Herr Koch, and Stepan are still speechless.

"Tell them you're Ukrainian," Myron finally says in Ukrainian. He puts his hands on his hips.

Stepan shakes his head. "They'll send us back behind Soviet lines."

Myron looks as if he is about to take action. "There are Ukrainian diasporas in America. Churches and communities we can write to. We'll ask for sponsors. We can't lose our artists to the Communists." He jerks his head at Olena. "Or our writers, our composers. I'll make a plea. I'll find help. Ask the Americans for help. If you're Polish, they'll send you back to Poland. And Poland will send you back to Ukraine."

Stepan is confused, but Myron talks in low tones, confident —he knows this will work, he says—and he helps Stepan gather up the few belongings the Lucyks have. He opens Stepan's painting case, and Stepan stops at the bed.

How many times have they been shown mercy? How many people have helped them along the way? Olena's friends, who arranged his release from prison in L'viv. Tosia, who took them into the hunting lodge in the Carpathians. The Hungarian partisans, who camped in the yard and taught the boys how to make goulash over the fire. The Czechoslovakian villagers, who provided them a home and the commission to renovate the frescoes in their chapel in return for food. Commander Luger. The woman with buttered buns, and the driver of the funny bus. The artists in Berlin. The artists here in Bavaria. The Kochs. Frau Wechsel. Why not? Why not the Americans?

He calls Herr Koch over. He begins removing some of the paintings and sketches. He has worked on a few new canvases. He leans the sketches on the window, along the floor. Watzemann. Chiemsee. Berchtesgaden. A farm. He says to Myron, "Tell Koch and Frau Wechsel that they should each choose some paintings. As a thank-you and to remember us by."

He busies himself to hold back the tears, stops selecting, and simply puts all the paintings out.

Herr Koch stands with his arms folded, emotion rippling over his wrinkled face. Frau Wechsel comments on the beauty of the paintings, saying she cannot possibly take one. Stepan tells her to take two. He lifts one from Königssee, holds it out to Koch. Koch smiles, but he points to the window.

Stepan turns to see which one he wants. It is two women in a field, wearing embroidered blouses in green and gold and red. Restored from his memory.

"Poland?" Koch asks.

Stepan sees Olena and Tosia in the doorway. The children are shifting next to them, each with chocolate stains on their hands and faces.

"No," Stepan says and hands him the two women. "Galicia. We are Ukrainians."

NOTES ABOUT THE STORIES

Souvenirs from Kyiv

This story was the 2nd Place Winner of the HNS International Short Story Award 2014 and appeared in the anthology, *Distant Echoes: stories of people, places and times past by writers from the Historical Novel Society*. Originally titled *Souvenirs from Kiev*, I wrote it five months after I had published my first novel. I was filled to the brim with anecdotes and research and this story flowed out like a river. Larissa's voice was so strong, she could not be ignored.

The Partisans: Part One—Mykhailo

This story is an excerpt and rewrite of a chapter from my first novel, *Deep Wells, Burning Forests*. Based on my great uncle Mykhailo's personal accounts when he and his men floated into one partisan army after another, sometimes collaborating with the Germans, sometimes with the Yugoslavians. His journey took him to eastern Austria, and then to Augsburg, Germany. He passed away at the age of 101 in December 2019.

The Partisans: Part Two—Marusia

My maternal grandmother, Maria, was involved in the OUN during Polish occupation of their territory and was well groomed for fighting in the resistance. Her journey is as exceptional as can be. She was a nurse for some time, following her brothers as far as she could. They were all eventually split up by circumstances. My grandmother fled through the Alps of Austria with the Soviets just behind her. After marching through the mountains in deep snows in March, she and her companions were picked up by an American military transport. She met my grandfather at a DP camp in Salzburg, where my mother was born. Maria was reunited with her brother, Peter, there as well. Together, they found Mykhailo in Augsburg.

The Partisans: Part Three—Danylo

My great uncle Pete (Mykhailo and Maria's youngest brother) is the inspiration for this story. He was the most forthcoming in his retellings and he told me his adventures like a true storyteller. We laughed, we cried, we reflected. He also served me the strangest homemade liquor out of a vodka bottle. It was brown, like cognac.

From Before to After-After

Ludmilla Boiko Karkoc (Lida) was my godmother (married to my Great Uncle Pete). Although it is not explicitly stated exactly how old she is in this story, I did make her more aware and mature than the five years old she was when her parents and she were first deported from Kyiv to a German labor camp. Her father was a Communist. She was not sure which camp they had stayed in but assumed it was somewhere near the Polish-German border.

After much research, I placed her in Wilhelmshagen and built in my father's story about his experiences in that labor camp, as her memories sounded similar to my father's. She mentioned that there was a school aimed at the Germanification of young children, which Wilhelmshagen also had.

Yurko and his near-death experience from starvation in this story is based on my father's retellings about that experience. The probability that my godmother (who married into my mother's side of the family) and my father ever meeting anywhere within the two fronts are probably very unlikely but I wanted to capture their labor camp experiences in this story.

Ludmilla was nearly killed in an explosion when the camp guards dropped her mother and her into those pits as described in this story. The Soviets attacked the area and eventually liberated her camp. She and her mother fled through the forest though Ludmilla was terribly shell-shocked. They found a town where Ludmilla and her mother were taken in by a German woman, and Ludmilla attended school there. The story about the coffee and the doll are also based on what she told me. Her mother's plan was to stay put so that they could eventually find Ludmilla's father after the war. And they did but not until quite some time after the war.

. . .

An Inventory of Mercies

This story is dedicated to the Lucyk side of the family. The events depicted here were shared by my father, Yurij (Yurko) Raphael Lucyk, who had an amazing recollection of the events. My grandfather, Stepan Lucyk, was a well-known painter, who had studied in Paris and had a vast network of artists and dissidents living in Europe's Ukrainian diasporas. Those people helped to save the family, and orchestrated their escape from Wilhelmshagen (they had only been given permission to see a doctor in the nearby village and were picked up by artists friends and taken to safety). My grandmother was a writer and composer. My great aunt Tosia was a teacher, an activist and, eventually, a very good spy. After writing these short stories, I knew I had one more story to tell about my family. *The Woman at the Gates* features my great aunt and my grandmother, and I have built in many other family anecdotes into the novel.

A LETTER FROM CHRYSTYNA

Dear reader,

I want to say a huge thank you for choosing to read *Souvenirs from Kyiv*. If you did enjoy it, and want to keep up to date with all my latest releases, just sign up at the following link. Your email address will never be shared and you can unsubscribe at any time.

www.bookouture.com/chrystyna-lucyk-berger

You can also subscribe to my newsletter and receive a free copy of *Historical and Cultural Essays on WW2 Ukraine: A Companion Guide to Souvenirs from Kyiv and The Woman at the Gates*. I go into more historical details as well as which of the true stories inspired the events in my works. You'll be immediately involved in my projects and be kept up to date on new releases, beta reading opportunities, advanced review copies, plus my historical and cultural background blog relating to my research, my travels, and my experiences while writing.

I hope you loved *Souvenirs from Kyiv* and if you did I would be very grateful if you could write a review. I'd love to hear what you think, and it makes such a difference helping new readers to discover one of my books for the first time. Your feedback also helps me to develop as an author.

Thank you so much and I look forward to hearing from you,

Chrystyna Lucyk-Berger

www.inktreks.com

GLOSSARY

All names, except for those of the major historical personas and those long-since gone, are fictional. I have provided foreign-word definitions in the glossary, used the spelling of the Ukrainian and Slavic languages as listed in the *Slavic Cataloging Manual* whenever possible, and kept all geographical names as true as could be, using the names as they were listed in the indexes and maps or as they were more commonly known in that time period except for the spelling of Kyiv. *Souvenirs from Kiev* was the title of the first published edition and reflected the historically accurate spelling of Ukraine's capital city. When my publisher approached me with the offer to take up the anthology, we quickly decided to change the title of the collection and the title story to *Souvenirs from Kyiv*. It is our nod to Ukraine's fragile fight for independence and sovereignty; our way of recognizing the native Ukrainian language.

bat'ko/bat'ku
father

Bürgermeister
mayor

chystka
purge. The intelligentsia (the educated and skilled people who posed a threat to an oppressed Communist society) were the target of these chystkas. They were systematically sent to labor camps or simply executed by the Communist secret police.

Dirndel
traditional Austrian dress

Gestapo
Hitler's secret police

Gymnasium
high school/college preparatory

Herr Oberst
German officer rank, equiv. to Colonel

horilka
alcohol, spirits

Kulka
Pellet: the codename for Danylo Hanchar

Lys
Fox: the codename for Mykhailo Hanchar

medivka
a spirit made of potato mash and honey

Most
a hard apple cider

nashi
ours, as in "our people"

Nimaky/Nimtsi
Ukrainian words for Germans

NKVD
Soviet secret police

Obstler
spirit brewed with a mixture of orchard fruits

Ostarbeiter
Eastern workers. As ordered by Hitler, workers from the East
were "recruited" to work camps in Germany and other coun-
tries in occupied Western Europe.

OUN
Organization of Ukrainian Nationalists. An underground political group formed to maintain national consciousness under the
oppressive Polish and Russian regimes. It was founded by a host
of Ukrainian émigrés after World War I and headed by Andrij
Mel'nyk but fractured into the OUN-M and OUN-B, the latter
of which was headed by the ultra-nationalist Stepan Bandera.

pani
Mrs.

pan
Mr.

panna
Miss/Ms.

Reichskanzlei
Third Reich Headquarters for the region

SD
security service of the SS

selo
village

Soldatenheim
soldier's home

tato/tatu
father

titka
aunt

UPA
Ukraiins'ka Povstans'ka Armiia—Ukrainian Insurgent Army

Wehrmacht
German forces